Dendera, Temple of Time

"José María Barrera presents a very clear depiction of the color ceiling in the pronaos of the Hathor temple at Dendera. Brilliant photographs are accompanied by the precise locations. A detailed high-quality overview of the complete ceiling includes panels and architrave undersides. This book's main subject is the description of all the figures depicted at the panels of the ceiling, which are a representation of the old Egyptian calendar and sky visualizations of the Greco-Roman time in Egypt. These not only represent genuine traditional old Egyptian gods of time and the known celestial bodies but also the inclusion of the zodiacal signs of Babylonian-Greco origin. This is an exceptionally well-suited introduction into early astronomy and concepts of time of this advanced civilization for non-professionals and professionals likewise."

DANIELA MENDEL-LEITZ, PH.D., ACADEMIC STAFF MEMBER FOR THE
INSTITUTE FOR ANCIENT NEAR EASTERN STUDIES (IANES) AT TÜBINGEN UNIVERSITY

"A wonderfully illustrated book that gives an excellent overview of the decoration on the ceiling of the pronaos at Dendera."

GYULA PRISKIN, PH.D., AUTHOR OF THE ANCIENT EGYPTIAN BOOK OF THE MOON AND
SENIOR LECTURER AT THE DEPARTMENT OF ANCIENT HISTORY, UNIVERSITY OF SZEGED

"Behold a timeless tome, where the celestial tapestry depicted on the ceiling of the pronaos inside the ancient Egyptian temple at Dendera unfolds, woven with astrological threads by the remarkable author José María Barrera in this captivating work of scholarly allure. Finally! A book that unravels the entire ethereal procession of ancient Egyptian gods sailing through the night sky. With resplendent high-resolution photographs and meticulous research, Barrera unveils the profound connection between the cosmos and humanity and the stars as depicted on the ancient temple's ceiling, unveiling the meaning concealed within."

ANYEXTEE, FILMMAKER AND AUTHOR OF
THE ADEPT INITIATE'S GUIDE TO THE LUXOR TEMPLE

"A book of astonishing beauty! A before and after in our vision of ancient Egyptian skies through the astronomical ceiling of the Hypostyle Hall of the Temple of Dendera. Barrera will not disappoint anyone."

JUAN ANTONIO BELMONTE AVILÉS, RESEARCH PROFESSOR OF ASTRONOMY
AT THE INSTITUTO DE ASTROFÍSICA DE CANARIAS

"A triumph of historical splendor. Not only does José María Barrera expose us to the glorious living color of Egyptian antiquity, but his expert photographic re-creations and learned text elucidate the mysteries and encrypted ideas of the ceiling of the Temple of Dendera like no other work available."

MITCH HOROWITZ, PEN AWARD–WINNING AUTHOR OF
OCCULT AMERICA AND *UNCERTAIN PLACES*

"This book with its clear and beautiful pictures allows its reader to perceive and admire all the details of the reliefs, even those that are usually hidden from the naked eye. It was like seeing Dendera for the first time again."

MANON Y. SCHUTZ, PH.D., LECTURER AND TEACHING
AND RESEARCH FELLOW AT THE UNIVERSITY OF MÜNSTER

"Ancient Egyptians thoroughly understood the 26,000-year cycle of the twelve 2,160-year Great Ages. They recorded this sacred record of time on the exquisite ceiling of the Dendera temple, and *now José María Barrera has decoded it!* The Egyptians taught the people to live according to this harmony for thousands of years—the attunement we need for survival. Read José María Barrera's book!"

BARBARA HAND CLOW, AUTHOR OF
ASTROLOGY AND THE RISING OF KUNDALINI AND *THE PLEIADIAN AGENDA*

"Finding the right words to describe the Temple of Hathor at Dendera is nigh impossible. José María Barrera has achieved it in this valuable pictorial study of the Hypostyle Hall ceiling when he concluded that it 'should not exist, yet does indeed exist.' For many reasons, I totally agree with him."

CHRISTOPHER DUNN, AUTHOR OF
LOST TECHNOLOGIES OF ANCIENT EGYPT AND *GIZA: THE TESLA CONNECTION*

"A great artist who presents different parts of the Dendera temple for the modern eye."

AHMED OSMAN, AUTHOR OF
THE EGYPTIAN ORIGINS OF KING DAVID AND THE TEMPLE OF SOLOMON

Dendera, Temple of Time

The Celestial Wisdom of Ancient Egypt

José María Barrera

Inner Traditions

Rochester, Vermont

Inner Traditions
One Park Street
Rochester, Vermont 05767
www.InnerTraditions.com

Cataloging-in-Publication Data for this title is available from the Library of Congress

ISBN 978-1-64411-834-4 (print)
ISBN 978-1-64411-835-1 (ebook)

Printed and bound in in China by Reliance Printing Co., Ltd

10 9 8 7 6 5 4 3 2 1

Text design and layout by Debbie Glogover and Kenleigh Manseau
This book was typeset in Garamond Premier Pro with Noyh Geometric and Serat used as display typefaces

To send correspondence to the author of this book, mail a first-class letter to the author c/o Inner Traditions • Bear & Company, One Park Street, Rochester, VT 05767, and we will forward the communication, or contact the author directly at **www.josemariabarrera.com** or **barrerajose@yahoo.com**.

Eighteen months ago, while having breakfast, I mentioned to
my wife that I had the idea to go to Dendera and digitally
reconstruct the ceiling of its pronaos. She thought I was crazy,
but as always, she has given me her unconditional support.
Maryluz is my muse, the mirror that lets me see the bad
and the good. She is my Hathor.

Contents

Foreword

This is a remarkable book about a remarkable temple by a remarkable man. The temple of Dendera is one of the best preserved of all the ancient Egyptian temples. This is partly because it is one of the most recent, built at the end of Egypt's long history. Begun toward the end of the period of Greek rule (the Ptolemaic Period) and completed by the Romans, it was dedicated to the goddess Hathor, but Hathor is not the main character in this book. Rather, the star of the book is one of the most mysterious aspects of the temple—a spectacular ceiling that is the ancient Egyptian version of Stephen Hawking's *A Brief History of Time*. It is a ceiling that reveals how the universe began and how time was measured ever since by the ancient Egyptians.

For decades I have guided groups through Dendera and its wonderful architecture—the colossal Hathor-headed columns, the dimly lit stairway where priests brought cult objects to the roof for religious celebrations, the scene of Isis resurrecting her husband, Osiris, from the dead. We try to see it all, but the highlight is the ceiling that is the subject of this book. Once we enter into the temple from the open courtyard, we are greeted by massive columns, each with the head of Hathor. We are in a room called the pronaos because it comes before the naos, the shrine that held the statue of the goddess Hathor inside the Holy of Holies. These huge columns support our mysterious ceiling. Inevitably, my groups look up and are dazzled by the beautiful, vivid colors revealed by a recent cleaning by the Egyptian Antiquities Service. The groups are always surprised to learn that the color is all original. Nothing has been repainted.

Once the group is over its color-shock, the fun begins. The group keeps looking up at the ceiling more than 50 feet above us and try to make out what is going on. First, we discern boats with gods in them that seem to be sailing in a procession of some sort. Then we notice that many of the gods have stars on their heads, others the solar disk. As the group tries to figure out the story line, someone usually notices what looks like Taurus the bull. Then someone sees Cancer the crab, and we realize it is a celestial ceiling. The astronomer-priests of ancient Egypt are showing us how they viewed the sky. But that's where it ends. We have to move on to see the rest of the temple. We have had a wonderful but incomplete experience. We never find out who these gods in the boats are. Where are they going? Who is that ram with four wings? We never get answers. Now, with this book that you have in your hands, you have all the answers. How this came about is almost as remarkable as the ceiling and involves our remarkable author.

On his first trip to Egypt, José Barrera became obsessed with the same questions my groups always have. Who are those strange gods and what is going on? Unlike my groups, he returned, determined to find the answers. For three intense days he took more than 5,000 high-resolution photographs of the ceiling. When he returned to the United States, he wrote a software program that enabled him to stitch together the photographs to give a clear, unbroken picture of the entire celestial ceiling. Then he did his homework, researching scholarly texts to find out who are those snakes pulling the divine boat across the sky, why is there a child sucking his thumb inside a solar disk? It is wonderful to finally know who all those gods are, but the real payoff is that the reader also learns what the ceiling is about—Time! The ceiling shows us how the Egyptians viewed and measured time. Those gods and goddesses with the stars on their heads are the 12 hours of the night. Then there are the decans—the 36 constellations that rotate through the night sky during the year, a different one appearing on the horizon every 10 days, marking 36 weeks of 10 days each. This gave the Egyptians a 360-day year, but soon their astronomers realized that the calendar was out of phase with the natural world by 5 days, so they added five extra days, the epagomenal days. The Dendera ceiling has it all, even the gods of the five extra days.

Any civilization that lasted 3,000 years can be expected to have a deep sense of time, and that is what this book conveys. We see the Egyptian fascination with and dependence on the seasons, their obsession with the measurement of time, and all the gods and goddesses who participated in the relentless march of time. It is all here for you to discover. Enjoy the journey.

BOB BRIER

SENIOR RESEARCH FELLOW, LONG ISLAND UNIVERSITY

BOB BRIER is an author, lecturer, and world-renowned expert in Egyptology. A Senior Research Fellow at Long Island University, he has appeared in Discovery Channel and Learning Channel documentaries and is a leading researcher on mummification practices from around the globe.

Acknowledgments

I want to express gratitude to several individuals who have been instrumental in the completion and success of this book. First and foremost, I extend my deepest appreciation to my parents, Eduardo and Patsy, for their unwavering belief in me and their invaluable feedback on the book.

I am also immensely grateful to my dear friends Joe Ahearn and Simon Young, who provided invaluable feedback on the early drafts of the book.

Additionally, I owe a great deal of thanks to Dr. Juan Antonio Belmonte, who generously shared his time and expertise, which proved invaluable in validating and correcting astronomical and calendric concepts.

I want to express my thanks to Dr. Daniela Mendel-Leitz and her husband Dr. Christian Leitz for their time in meeting me in New York, their wise counsel, their patient responses to my many queries, and the incredible book they sent me from Germany.

The comments and research provided by Dr. Gyula Priskin on the lunar scenes in the ceiling were immensely helpful.

Dr. Manon Y. Schutz also deserves my heartfelt appreciation for her patience in reading the manuscript, identifying deities, and helping me avoid amateur mistakes.

I cannot forget to acknowledge Isabella Anderson's outstanding editing and proofreading efforts, which were instrumental in helping this book reach its publication journey.

I would like to extend my sincere gratitude to Kim Brandt and Jake Warthon for their generous contributions of time and invaluable advice.

Finally, I am deeply grateful to Dr. Bob Brier for the kind words he wrote in the foreword of this book.

Note to the Reader

As with many stories from Egypt, the story of how the ancient Egyptian language was lost and found is a captivating tale.

During the final days of the Egyptian civilization, under the dominion of the Roman Empire, the ancient Egyptian language was confined to the use of priests within their temples. As their religious practices gradually declined, their language also slowly vanished and remained forgotten for over fifteen centuries. However, in the early nineteenth century, the fortuitous discovery of the Rosetta Stone enabled the resurrection of the ancient Egyptian language—well, almost.

Just like Hebrew or Arabic, ancient Egyptians wrote the consonants and left out the vowels in their scripts. As the language died, its sound faded with it. Imagine for a moment that English was written using only consonants. In such case the word "trumpet" would be written "trmpt." If English became a dead language, future Englishtologists would speculate if we pronounced "trmpt" like "trampot," "trumpat," or "trempot," and so on.

Thanks to Coptic, a direct descendant of ancient Egyptian, linguists and Egyptologists have been able to make many educated guesses on how the language sounded, but in plenty of cases, scholars are far from certain.

To ease the pronunciation of rows of consonants (a gift only given to the Polish), Egyptologists insert vowels between the consonants to make words more readable. Depending on their nationality, they Latinize the Egyptian in different ways. For example, English speaking Egyptologists use "U" or "W," while French Egyptologists use "OU."

In a poetic way, ancient Egyptians applied to their language the same technique they used to preserve their ancestors. Just as they removed the vital organs before mummifying the inert bodies, they removed the vowels from the consonants in their hieroglyphs, preserving them for eternity.

The names and inscriptions on the ceiling used throughout the book are based on the work in French of Sylvie Cauville, a remarkable Egyptologist who has devoted her career to the study of the Dendera temple complex. All her translations can be found in her book *Dendara XV, Traduction* (Cauville 2013a). I have made an effort to anglicize the francized names used by Cauville, so they are easier for the reader to consume.

Introduction

On a winter afternoon half a decade ago, my family and I passed in front of an exhibition of King Tutankhamun on Fifth Avenue in Manhattan. It looked like a tourist trap, but we decided to take shelter from the cold and enter the show.

The exhibit turned out to be an identical reproduction of Tutankhamun's tomb as found by Howard Carter in 1922 in the Valley of the Kings. The beauty of the objects, the vibrant colors, the sarcophagi, the masks, and the mysterious aura produced by the hieroglyph-covered walls left a deep impression on me that afternoon. Five months later, we visited Egypt.

Egypt makes us feel tiny. Its ancient ruins force us to think about how short our lives are, compared to human history. The enormous dimensions of the monuments turn us into minute figures in the presence of mysterious and forgotten ancient gods. Walls covered with incomprehensible signs make our ignorance evident, and the solemnity and grace of the architecture suggest how wise and advanced this ancient civilization was.

Of all the places that this wonderful country has to offer, the one that struck me the most was the great Temple of Dendera. Unlike Ephesus in Turkey, the Parthenon in Greece, or the Forum in Rome, where only traces of the buildings still stand and visitors are forced to imagine their past grandeur, the Temple of Dendera is perfectly preserved thanks both to the dryness of the desert and to the sand that had buried it for centuries.

The construction of this quiet temple dates to the Ptolemaic period, more than two thousand years ago.

I vividly remember the spectacular feeling I experienced upon entering the temple's front portico, its pronaos, and looking up and seeing the enigmatic and colorful astral figures on the ceiling that was supported by huge columns crowned with the face of Hathor, the patron goddess of the temple.

Similar in size to that of the Sistine Chapel, the ceiling of the pronaos in the Temple of Dendera not only embodies most of the astronomical knowledge of its ancient creators but—even further—the graceful contours of the figures, the intricately worked patterns of their clothing, and the thousands of hieroglyphs that surround the characters all combine to create a stunningly complex and yet completely harmonious panoply of breathtaking beauty. It is inarguably one of the great artistic achievements of humankind.

The temple's more recent history is as fascinating as its ancient beginnings. In the late eighteenth century, the savants of the Napoleonic expedition to Egypt found it about thirty miles north of Luxor, buried up to its waist in sand. At that time, humanity had forgotten how to read the pictorial writings of the ancient Egyptians. The visiting French adventurers resorted to references given by ancient Greek and Roman visitors, who spoke of a remarkable ancient civilization.

What made the Temple of Dendera so special to these French scholars were the familiar figures found among thousands of indecipherable messages on its ceiling: the signs of the zodiac. These symbols were one of the few points of recognition between Western visitors and this strange and forgotten civilization. Their findings naturally aroused great interest across Europe. Twenty-five years later, in 1821, a delegation was sent to remove the roof from one of the temple's chapels and transport it to France. Today, what is known as the Dendera Circular Zodiac is housed in the Louvre Museum in Paris.

One of the most renowned members of the Napoleonic expedition, Baron Vivant Denon, recounted his impressions when he first arrived at the Temple of Dendera, then known to the French by its Greek name, Tentyra:

> I despair of being able to express all that I felt on standing under the portico of Tentyra. I felt that I was in the sanctuary of the arts and sciences. How many periods presented themselves to my imagination at the sight of such an edifice! How many ages of creative ingenuity were requisite to bring a nation to such a degree of perfection and sublimity in the arts! . . . I could not expect to find any thing in Egypt more complete, more perfect, than Tentyra; I was confused by the multiplicity of objects, astonished by their novelty, and tormented by the fear of never again visiting them. On casting my eyes on the ceilings I had perceived zodiacs, planetary systems, and celestial planispheres, represented in a tasteful arrangement; the walls I had observed to

be covered with groups of pictures exhibiting the religious rites of this people, their labours in agriculture and the arts, and their moral precepts. I saw that the Supreme Being, the first cause, was everywhere depicted by the emblems of his attributes; every thing was equally important for my pencil, and I had but a few hours to examine, to reflect on, and to copy what it had been the labour of ages to conceive, to put together, and to decorate. (Denon 1803)

For several years after that first memorable visit with my family, I endeavored to make sense of this most remarkable place. Sadly, I discovered that literature about the Temple of Dendera was scarce, and not very affordable. Most of the books I found were academic treatises written in French or German. The internet offered hundreds of images of varying degrees of quality, but to my surprise, there existed no systematic reconstruction of the entire ceiling in high resolution. Imagine if that were the case for the Sistine Chapel!

My desire to understand the story that the ceiling was trying to tell (and, I must admit, my wish to be in its presence once again) led to my return to Egypt in April of 2021. I proceeded to spend days at the temple, examining the ceiling through a telephoto lens and capturing the images on a high-end digital camera. In the end, I amassed over five thousand photographs and developed specialized software to stitch them together, creating a unique panoramic view of the entire ceiling in all its grandeur.

This book is not intended to be an academic work. It is the attempt of an engineer obsessed with language, cognition, symbology, and time. My goal is to try to convey the awe and admiration I felt underneath the ceiling of the temple. It is an homage to the goddess Hathor and the thousands of artists and workers who made this place possible. In presenting the images, I have humbly ventured to add some historical and mythological context that I feel helps one to appreciate this masterpiece in its full magnificence.

The Land of Cycles

The Nile River crosses northern Africa's desert lands, forming a long and narrow oasis on its banks. It is here where, despite the brutal conditions of their environment, the people of Egypt managed to create the most enduring civilization in history. Every year between June and September, the waters of the heavy summer rains and the thawing of snow from the Ethiopian mountains descend toward Egypt loaded with fertilizing sediments. They cause the river to overflow into the desert, creating some of the most fertile lands on the planet, in stark contrast to its arid surroundings.

Egyptians lived at the mercy of the river's annual ebb and flow. During the years of opportune flooding, harvests were bountiful and brought abundance and prosperity. Pharaohs taxed the surplus wealth, strengthening and prolonging their dynasties. If the flooding was poor, the crops along the Nile were likewise poor, and segments of the population starved. On the other hand, if the rainfall in upstream Ethiopia was excessive, the resulting floods were catastrophic, devastating the cities along the river, spoiling their crops, and drowning their people. Severe drought or extreme inundation brought famine and social unrest. The two things Egyptians feared most about their vital river were too little water and too much of it.

The history of ancient Egypt is characterized by long periods of prosperity and political stability roughly corresponding to periods of regular flooding, interrupted by the so-called "Intermediate Periods" of political struggle loosely matching periods of abnormal water levels.

Given the Nile's variability, state policy was calibrated so as to minimize the suffering during bad years and to maximize the yield in good years. The book of Genesis illustrates this civic response in the parable of Joseph and the Pharaoh's dream:

Seven years of great abundance are coming throughout the land of Egypt, but seven years of famine will follow them. Then all the abundance in Egypt will be forgotten, and the famine will ravage the land. The abundance in the land will not be remembered, because the famine that follows it will be so severe. . . . Let Pharaoh appoint commissioners over the land to take a fifth of the harvest of Egypt during the seven years of abundance. They should collect all the food of these good years that are coming and store up the grain under the authority of Pharaoh, to be kept in the cities for food. This food should be held in reserve for the country, to be used during the seven years of famine that will come upon Egypt, so that the country may not be ruined by the famine. (Genesis 41:29–36, NIV)

The impact of the Nile's annual ebb and flow on the Egyptian worldview cannot be overstated. This centrality is reflected in the story of Osiris, the seminal myth of ancient Egyptian religion. Osiris, god of fertility, is dismembered by his brother Seth, the beast-headed god of the desert and disorder. Isis, sister-wife of Osiris, reconstitutes his body and uses her magic to bring him back to life as god of the underworld. To the Egyptians, Osiris's death and subsequent resurrection by Isis represented the annual cycle of nature and the Nile, as described by Diodorus of Sicily, a Greek historian from the first century BCE:

These two gods, they hold, regulate the entire universe, giving both nourishment and increase to all things by means of a system of three seasons which complete the full cycle through an unobservable movement, these being spring and summer and winter; and these seasons, though in nature most opposed to one another, complete the cycle of the year in the fullest harmony. (Diodorus tr. 1933)

Just as the Egyptians perceived the annual dance between flood and drought, they understood the cycle of day and night as a struggle between light and darkness. The sun god Re descends daily to the underworld (the Duat) at dusk, where he begins his twelve-hour journey eastward, fighting Apep, the malefic force of darkness. Each day, Re defeats Apep and is brilliantly resurrected at dawn.

The Egyptian myths can be seen as rhetorical devices to explain the patterns of nature and its cycles. Humanized stories were used to narrate the interactions between the antagonistic forces that surrounded them, like the river and the desert, life and death, growth and decay, chaos and order. Their theriocephalic deities (hybrid creatures with human bodies and animal heads) were the symbols they used to represent the natural forces and principles that underlay reality.

Osiris as the moon at the apex of the lunar cycle between his two sisters, Nephthys (on the left, who represents decline) and Isis (who represents growth). Notice Isis releasing the ankh ♀ (the vital force) and giving it to Osiris while Nephthys holds her ankh locked on her staff, marking the turn of the cycle.

The Temples of Egypt

The temples of Egypt were constructed not only as religious centers but were also intimately intertwined with many aspects of society. The temple was an essential economic, political, medical, and educational entity.

From their beginnings around the fourth millennium BCE, hundreds of temples were built in scores of cities until the sun finally set on this ancient civilization during the early ascendancy of the Roman Empire. Temples were multigenerational projects enhanced, restored, and rebuilt by successive dynasties across centuries. Their size and opulence depended on the opulence and political prominence of the cities where they were founded.

Temples were the homes of the gods and, critically, the gods' portals to the mortal world. The Egyptian temple represented the universe—its ceiling was the sky, its floor and columns were the earth and the trees, and its crypts were the underworld. Priests, mediators between the earthly and the divine, were in charge of the administration and the performance of the daily rituals at the temples. Access to the temple interior was reserved exclusively for those priests and for visiting pharaohs.

Egyptians referred to a temple as a "mansion of a god," and each of these mansions served as the earthly home of its deity, to which common people made a pilgrimage for the purpose of worship.

Broadly speaking, Egyptian temples fell into two main categories. The first was mortuary temples that were dedicated to specific pharaohs, each of whom became a god upon his demise. The Egyptians referred to such a temple as a "Mansion of Millions of Years" and used it as a shrine where the deceased pharaoh could be worshiped as a divine being. The Hatshepsut temple at Deir el-Bahari, constructed in the fifteenth century BCE, is an example of a mortuary temple.

The other category of temple was the cult temple dedicated to a specific deity. Prime examples of cult temples are the Temple of Horus at Edfu, the Temple of Isis at Philae, and, indeed, our very own Temple of Hathor at Dendera.

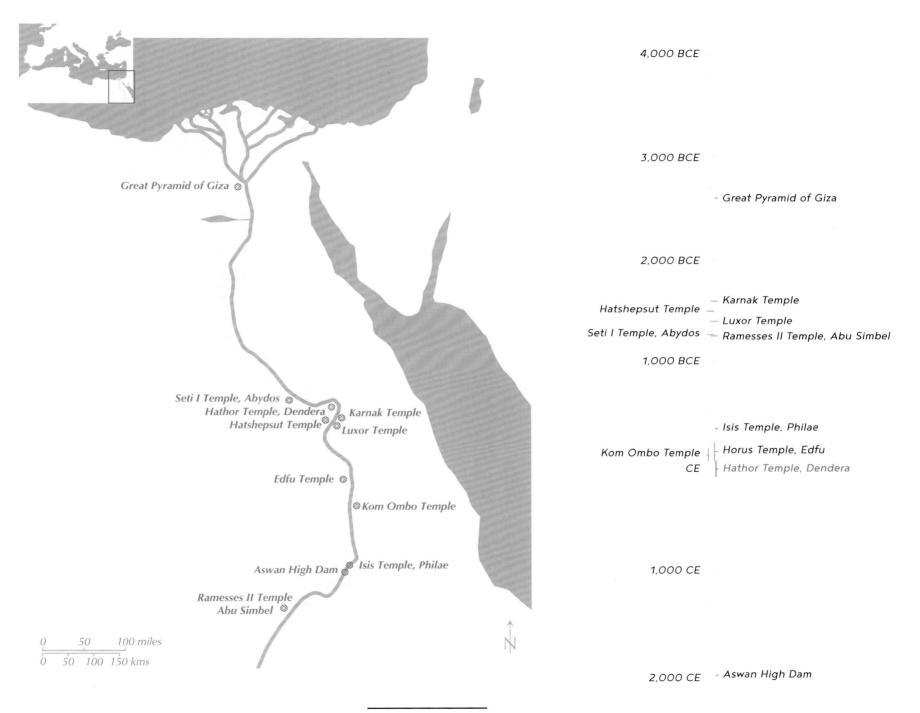

4,000 BCE

3,000 BCE

Great Pyramid of Giza

2,000 BCE

Karnak Temple

Hatshepsut Temple

Luxor Temple

Seti I Temple, Abydos   Ramesses II Temple, Abu Simbel

1,000 BCE

Isis Temple, Philae

Kom Ombo Temple   Horus Temple, Edfu

CE   Hathor Temple, Dendera

Great Pyramid of Giza

Seti I Temple, Abydos
Hathor Temple, Dendera   Karnak Temple
Hatshepsut Temple   Luxor Temple

Edfu Temple

Kom Ombo Temple

1,000 CE

Aswan High Dam   Isis Temple, Philae

Ramesses II Temple
Abu Simbel

2,000 CE   Aswan High Dam

0   50   100 miles
0   50   100   150 kms

N

Main monuments of Egypt in space and time.

The Astronomical Function of the Temples

The Nile's impact on the stability of society forced the Egyptians to look for ways to predict the time of the flooding and accurately measure the water levels at different times of the year. It should therefore come as no surprise that the all-important institution of the temple was involved in keeping an eye on the behavior of the great river.

The word *temple,* like the word *tempo,* comes from the Latin *tempus,* meaning "time," "period of time," or "season," which in turn derives from the Indo-European root *temp,* meaning "to extend," "to stretch," or "to measure."

The pharaoh and Seshat, the goddess of measurement, carefully determined the alignment of a new temple. This ceremony was called the "stretching of the cord" and it is attested in the walls of many temples. A cord was stretched between two poles establishing the central axis, and the four corners of the temple were set into place. A version of this cornerstone ceremony is a tradition practiced to this day, especially in establishing churches and public buildings such as courthouses and city halls.

One of the many functions of the temples was to serve as astronomical observatories. They were used to determine the dates of solstices and the beginning and end of different annual periods. One of the important activities in the temples was the measurement of the passing of time and the creation and regulation of calendars. Priests responsible for observing the sky wore panther skins adorned with stars and were called "Overseers of the Hours."

These astronomer-priests methodically observed the cosmic dome for recognizable configurations of stars and bright celestial bodies and created charts of their movements. They also studied the rhythms of natural phenomena and identified coinciding astral patterns. Priests used the stars as markers to foretell the corresponding natural events based on this knowledge of the heavens.

Celestial events were celebrated with festivals, which determined the agricultural and social activities for that particular time: plowing, sowing, harvesting, brewing, and so on. The priests modulated societal activity, synchronizing it to the natural cycles with these festivals and rituals commemorating those celestial events. Through this regulation of human behavior, the Egyptians tuned-up their civilization to the harmonies of their gods, which they called the *ntr* (anglicized as *netjer*).

They discovered that the annual flood corresponded with the first yearly appearance (heliacal rising) of the star Sirius, personified as the goddess Sopdet (conflated with Isis). It is said that her tears from mourning the death of her beloved husband and brother Osiris caused the flooding of the Nile.

Egyptians divided their year into three seasons of four months (called the *tetramenes*): the flooding season (*akhet*) from June to September, the growing season (*peret*) from October to February, and the harvesting season (*shemu*) from March to May.

Many of the temples were placed on the banks of the Nile and included a nilometer, a wall on the river with steps whose purpose was to measure the river's level throughout the year.

These measurements were then used to calibrate the taxes to be levied on the population. This natural economic indicator ensured that the tax burden was always appropriate to the times, and is one example of the environmental awareness that allowed the Egyptians to maintain a stable civilization that endured for more than four millennia.

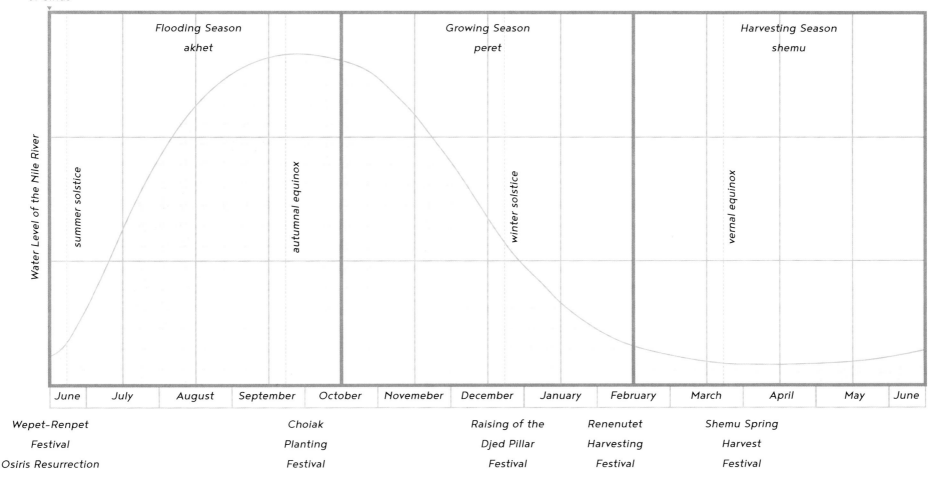

Egyptian ideal year: the flooding of the Nile, the seasons, and main festivals. The ancient Egyptian civil calendar had 360 days and an additional 5 epagomenal days (days of Thoth) for a total of 365 days every year. The actual solar year has around 365¼ days. Lacking the leap year, the Egyptian calendar drifted from the actual solar year, which made yearly events like the heliacal rising of Sirius or the equinoxes fall one day earlier every four years of the civil calendar. This meant that the dates of the festivals had to be adjusted or they became merely symbolic, having to introduce new festivals as centuries went by so that they corresponded to the actual events. See Belmonte Avilés 2012, chap. 2.

Measuring Time

The measurement of time is one of the most deeply rooted concepts in any society. The day has 24 hours, the week 7 days, the months around 30 days (some have more, others less), and the year has 365 days, but every four years, we have one more day in February.

We all use wristwatches or cellphones to see the hour of the day, and we use calendars to schedule all kinds of events. All these things come naturally to us, but imagine if our calendars and devices were to suddenly disappear. How would we go about conducting our daily business "on time"?

We take for granted these fundamental tools and concepts essential to the proper functioning of society.

Scheduling and planning are vital for any agricultural society, especially as you move further from the equator and the seasonal variability accentuates.

Ancient people realized that there were many unpredictable things on Earth, but they found order and regularity in the sky. Regardless of the eventualities of their mundane world, they were always able to count on reliable beings from above. The sun tirelessly set and rose. The moon waned and waxed while the constellations slowly but surely advanced through the celestial dome.

The first obvious unit of time is the day. We can count how many times the sun rises until the following winter. Unfortunately, the number of times Earth revolves around its axis does not precisely match the solar year (365.242 days). This discrepancy is why we add one day every four years, so the calendar doesn't get out of sync with the seasons.

The moon is another obvious source of periodicity, but it does not correspond to the solar year either. Twelve lunations (lunar rotations around Earth, lunar months) take 354.367 days. That is around eleven days short of the solar year.

Our planet is not perpendicular to its rotation axis. It is currently tilted 23½ degrees. This tilting oscillates from around 22 to 24 degrees every 40,000 years. During summer in the Northern Hemisphere, the north of the tilted axis points toward the sun, days are longer, and that hemisphere receives more solar radiation. In the Southern Hemisphere, the opposite occurs, and it is winter. As the year goes by in the north, days become shorter and colder until the shortest day of the year is reached on December 21, the winter solstice. Over the next six months, days become longer and warmer. Finally, the year's longest day arrives on June 21, the summer solstice. The word *solstice* comes from the Latin *solstitium,* from *sol* ("sun") + *sisto* ("standstill"). The equinoxes are the two days halfway between the solstices when the lengths of night and day are the same. The word *equinox* comes from the Latin *aequinoctium,* from *aequus* ("equal") + *nox* ("night").

The ecliptic is the apparent path followed by the sun over the year. It is called the ecliptic because it is where eclipses between the sun and the moon occur. The belt that extends around the ecliptic in which the paths of the planets and the moon fall is called the zodiac.

The constellations of the zodiac are twelve groups of bright stars on the ecliptic. These groups of stars form recognizable patterns typically associated with animals in antiquity—*zodiac* means "circle of little animals" in Greek, from the same root as "zoo."

The night sky seems to slowly rotate as Earth travels around the sun. Every year the constellations of the zodiac complete an entire cycle as viewed from Earth.

By looking at constellations during the year, humans learned to match them to the sun's annual cycle. In that way, they could anticipate the coming of the seasons depending on which stars were visible at night.

Owing to the wobble of Earth's axis of rotation, the zodiac constellation seen behind the sun at the vernal equinox slowly falls behind. This apparent retrograde motion of the sky is known as the equinoctial precession. One complete rotation takes around 26,000 years and is known as the Great Year. Therefore, the vernal equinox is in each of the twelve zodiacal constellations for about 2,166 years, known as an "astrological age." Starting around the fourth millennium BCE, the equinox was in Taurus for two millennia. Beginning in the second millennium BCE, it was in Aries. The equinox has been in Pisces for the last two thousand years, and now we are transitioning into the Age of Aquarius.

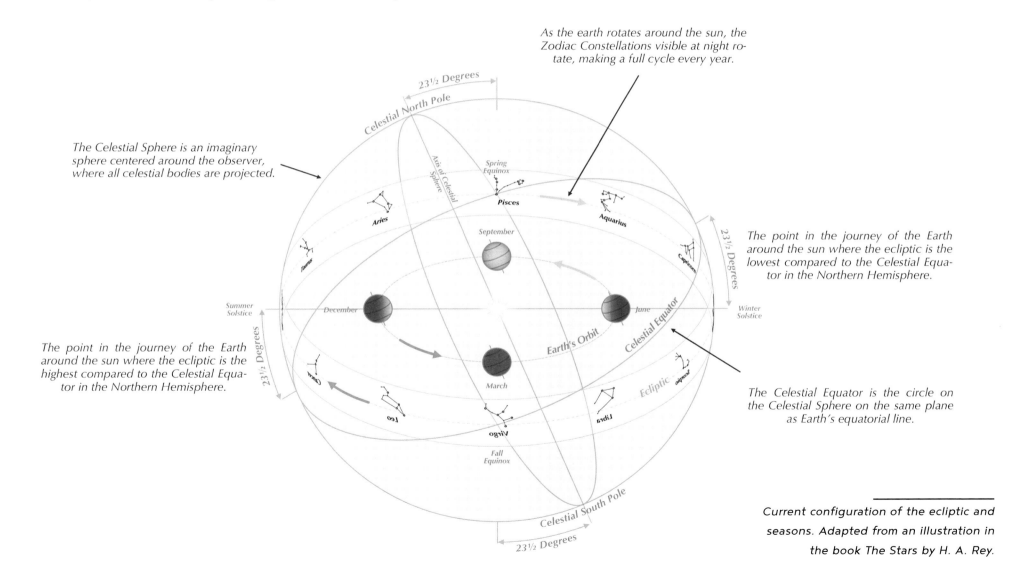

As the earth rotates around the sun, the Zodiac Constellations visible at night rotate, making a full cycle every year.

The Celestial Sphere is an imaginary sphere centered around the observer, where all celestial bodies are projected.

The point in the journey of the Earth around the sun where the ecliptic is the lowest compared to the Celestial Equator in the Northern Hemisphere.

The point in the journey of the Earth around the sun where the ecliptic is the highest compared to the Celestial Equator in the Northern Hemisphere.

The Celestial Equator is the circle on the Celestial Sphere on the same plane as Earth's equatorial line.

Current configuration of the ecliptic and seasons. Adapted from an illustration in the book The Stars by H. A. Rey.

Ancient Egyptian Astronomy

Complex societies require time measurement to coordinate social activities and the planning of agricultural cycles, even more so when the environmental conditions have extreme changes throughout the year, as was the case with the ancient Egyptians and the Nile's cycles of flooding and drought.

In the burning Egyptian desert, the star that dominated their myths was the sun. They conceived the sky as an ocean in which the sun sailed daily in a boat. Every evening the sun died on the horizon and descended into the underworld, where it traveled throughout the night and was reborn at dawn.

Their interest in the daily solar journey led them to develop the twenty-four-hour system—twelve daytime hours from dawn to dusk and twelve nighttime hours. Owing to Egypt's latitude north of the equator, the duration of day and night vary, forcing the ancient Egyptians to adjust the length of the hours throughout the year (unlike our hours that have a fixed length of sixty minutes).

During the day, they used obelisks and sundials to measure the hours. The oldest known gnomon (the part of a sundial that casts a shadow) dates back to 3500 BCE.

Likewise, they used water clocks and the stars during the night to measure time. The water clocks, called clepsydras (from the Greek, meaning "water thief"), were vessels with a small perforation through which the water dripped during the night. The hours were measured on scales engraved inside as the water level dropped. Egyptian clepsydras had different scales calibrated to follow the hours' varying durations over the year.

The Egyptians also devised a system of thirty-six asterisms (small constellations) to measure hours during the night, known as the decans. They noticed the rising and setting of the decans on the horizon and used them to measure the twelve hours at night. A new decan appears on the horizon at dawn every ten days, hence its name (from the Greek *déka,* "ten").

Ancient Egyptians developed a complex calendrical system to measure the year. The first Egyptian calendar was lunar and was maintained throughout the history of their ancient civilization and used by priests in religious celebrations and festivals.

The solar civil calendar was established in the Old Kingdom, consisting of twelve months of 30 days (360 days) and 5 additional days called the epagomenal days (see more about the epagomenal days on p. 73).

Sirius, the Dog Star, is the brightest star in the sky and was the most important star for the Egyptians, who knew it as Sopdet (called Sothis by the Greeks). The heliacal rising of Sirius corresponded to the beginning of the inundation of the Nile, marking the start of the Egyptian year.

Planets didn't play a major role in Egyptian astronomy. They knew the five planets visible to the naked eye and considered them as aspects of the god Horus.

Karl Richard Lepsius, a pioneering Prussian Egyptologist, discovered a memorial stone (stele) in 1881 at Tanis dating from 239 BCE. The stele contains what is known as the Decree of Canopus, an edict inscribed in three different scripts. There is a proposal in this decree to reform the calendar and introduce the leap year by adding a day at the end of the five epagomenal days every four years. For reasons that are not clear, the calendrical reform was not successful. Almost two centuries later, in 46 BCE, Julius Caesar modified the Roman calendar according to the Egyptian reform, giving rise to the Julian calendar.

The great Egyptian astronomical legacy was to divide the day into twenty-four hours and the year into 365 days. Their concepts of time were so powerful that the tempo of our lives still follow the rhythms they established thousands of years ago.

Star pattern on the sides of the central panel of the ceiling at the pronaos of the Dendera temple. The stars arranged in this pattern resemble a person stretching their arms and legs, with their "feet" standing eastward and their "heads" directed toward the west (Mendel 2022, 18).

The Temple of Hathor at Dendera

Time has been kind to the Temple of Dendera. When you enter the temple and see the bright colors of its ceiling, it is hard to believe that it has been standing for more than two thousand years.

A remarkable feature of Ptolemaic and Roman temples at the end of the Egyptian era is the information depicted on their walls from floor to ceiling. Priests, perhaps sensing the decline of their civilization, decided to carve on the surfaces of the temples knowledge previously unrecorded in order to preserve it for posterity.

Dendera, called *Iunet* by the ancient Egyptians and *Tentyris* (or Tentyra) by the Greeks, was an important religious center and capital of the sixth nome (the Greek term for their administrative districts) of Upper Egypt.

The main structure at Dendera is the temple of the millenary goddess Hathor. She was the sacred cow, the divine womb in which life grows, the deity of childbirth, fertility, and maternal love. She is the goddess of the rhythms of life and music, with the sistrum (a rattle) as one of her symbols and the instrument affiliated with her ceremonies. In her bovine form, she is a kind and nurturing mother. In her leonine form, she proved to be brutal and destructive.

Records attest to prior structures dedicated to the goddess Hathor on this site dating to 2500 BCE. The construction of the main body of the present temple, commissioned by Pharaoh Ptolemy XII, started in July of 54 BCE and lasted thirty-four years. After his passing in 51 BCE, his successor and daughter, Cleopatra VII, continued the construction work. The building of the temple's main house took place during the twenty-one years of her reign. Wall decorations had just started when she died in 30 BCE. Her image next to her son Caesarion can be seen on the temple's southern facade. After her death, Egypt became a Roman province, and Roman emperors, who are portrayed wearing Egyptian garments around the temple, continued the site's construction. The emperor Tiberius added the pronaos to the temple in the first century CE.

The Roman Imperial Crisis of the third century CE affected the maintenance of the temples, precipitating the decline of Egyptian religious institutions. Early Roman emperors were friendly toward the Egyptian religion. In contrast, the advent of Christian monotheism brought hostility and iconoclasm. A Christian basilica was built at the Dendera premises during the fifth century CE.

When the French savants from the Napoleonic expedition arrived in 1799, they found a centuries-old village established in the temple. It was half covered by sand carried by centuries of incessant desert winds. The famous "Zodiac of Dendera" was removed from one of the ceiling's chapels in 1821 and has become one of the jewels of the Louvre Museum, where it currently resides. The temple was fully cleared from sand by the French Egyptologist Auguste Mariette in 1895.

If it were not for the vandals and fanatics who, fearing the power of the temple's gods, decided to chisel out those gods' faces on walls and columns and for the zodiac removed by the French, the temple would be today just like it was when it was built.

Many centuries have passed since the last time priests solemnly chanted to the goddess. Today, many sparrows, permanent residents of the temple, fly around and sing, filling its spaces with life—a reminder that the spirit of Hathor still dwells there.

Description of the Temple

A massive mud-brick wall surrounds the ten acres of the Dendera temple complex. A gigantic gateway built by the emperor Domitian in 80 CE serves as the main entrance to the complex.

Besides its religious functions, the complex served as a place of pilgrimage and as a healing center where people received treatment for different illnesses. The site houses several structures, including a sacred lake, the Roman *mammisi* (birth house), the Christian basilica, the temple of Isis's birth, the *mammisi* of Mentuhotep II from the Eleventh Dynasty, and a sanatorium.

The Temple of Hathor is the main construction in the complex. Like other temples across Egypt, it is oriented to point toward the Nile. Because the river bends in this part, the temple runs north-south instead of east-west, which was usually the case. Its precise orientation is toward the heliacal rising of the star Alkaid, the tip of the tail of the Ursa Major constellation.

The temple was built from the inside out. The sanctuary was constructed first, followed by the surrounding chambers. The pronaos was added later by the Roman emperor Tiberius.

There are six Hathoric columns at the entrance of the temple, three on each side. The first room you encounter is the pronaos, whose ceiling is the subject of this book. The next room, housing six smaller columns, is called the "Hall of Appearances," as this was the chamber to which the statue of the goddess was taken from the sanctuary for ceremonies and processions.

The architecture of the temple is like a telescope along its central axis. As you walk deeper inside, the spaces become more gloomy, the ceilings lower and the floors higher, creating a more intimate atmosphere in the inner parts. Skylights on the ceilings of the multiple chambers allow the sun's rays to fall as spotlights on the walls. If you stand in one of the rooms for some time, you can see the light slowly moving, like a cursor, highlighting different sections on the wall. To my knowledge, the significance of this incredible feature has not been studied.

The most important room in the temple is the sanctuary—the sanctum sanctorum (holy of holies). It housed the boat used to carry the statue of the goddess during the processions. Only the pharaoh himself and a few high priests had access to this room. Around the central axis, there are a series of chapels dedicated to other deities and various chambers that served different ritual purposes.

There are six crypts underneath the temple that were used to store the sacred items, treasures, and archives. The most important object stored in the crypts was the statue of the goddess. A procession took the statue to a chapel on the roof the night before the New Year Festival, where it waited for the sun to rise so that it could be reunited with the solar disk. The crypts were also used to conduct initiatory rituals.

Finally, there are six so-called Osirian Chapels on the temple roof, where ceremonies for the god Osiris were performed under the moonlight.

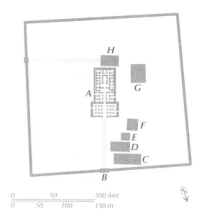

Dendera Temple Complex.

A Temple of Hathor
B Domitian Gate
C Roman Mammisi
D Christian Basilica
E Mammisi of Nectanebo I
F Sanatorium
G Sacred Lake
H Temple of Isis's birth as Sothis

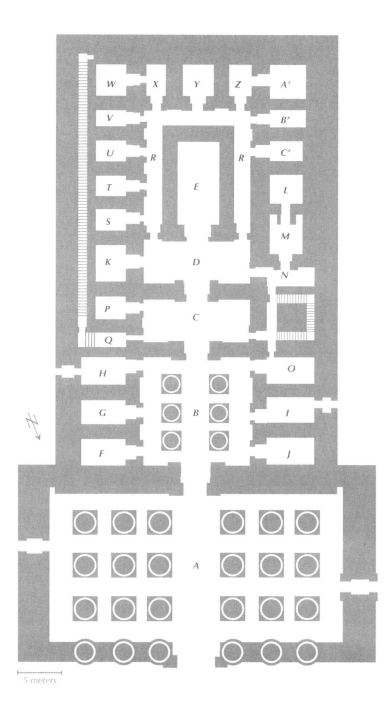

A Pronaos
B Hall of Appearances
C Offering Hall
D Ennead Hall
E Sanctuary
F Laboratory
G Storage Chamber
H Offering Chamber
I Hall of Appearances
J Treasury
K Textile Chamber
L The Pure Place
M Court of the First Feast
N Passage
O Access to Staircase
P Sacred Gallery
Q Staircase to Roof
R Hallway
S Shrine of the Nome of Dendera
T Shrine of Isis
U Shrine of Sokar
V Shrine of Harsomtus
W Shrine of Hathor's Sistrum
X Shrine of the Gods of Lower Egypt
Y Shrine of Hathor
Z Shrine of the Throne of Re
A' Shrine of Re
B' Shrine of the Menat Necklace
C' Shrine of Ihy

Temple of Hathor, main floor.

VUE DE LA PORTE DU NORD.

Gateway of Emperor Domitian, built in 80 CE. André Dutertre,
Description de l'Égypte, *vol. IV, plate 4.*

A.Vol.IV.

DENDERAH. (TENTYRIS.)

Pl.-.

VUE DE LA FAÇADE DU GRAND TEMPLE.

Facade of the Temple of Hathor. Notice the constructions by settlers on top of the temple. When the French expedition arrived to the site, it was covered in sand.
François-Charles Cécile, Description de l'Égypte, vol. IV, plate 7.

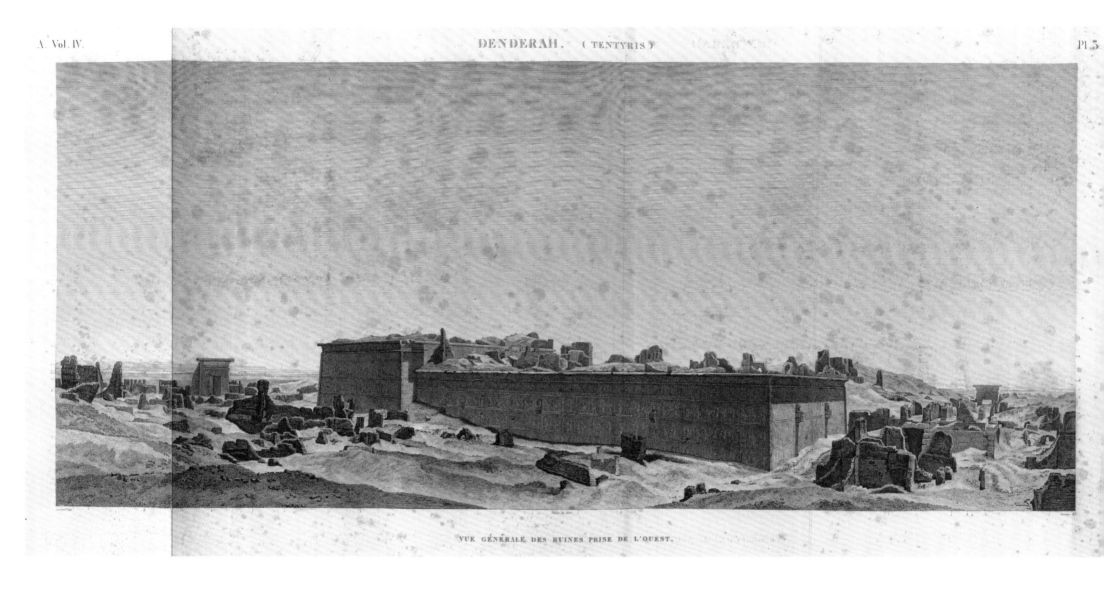

VUE GÉNÉRALE DES RUINES PRISE DE L'OUEST.

Temple view from the west.
André Dutertre, Description de l'Égypte, *vol. IV, plate 3.*

VUE PERSPECTIVE DE L'INTÉRIEUR DU PORTIQUE DU GRAND TEMPLE.

Depiction of a procession with statue of the goddess Hathor coming out of the pronaos. Jollois and de Villier, Description de l'Égypte, *vol. IV, plate 30.*

The Pronaos of the Temple

The first thing you see when approaching the Temple of Hathor from a distance is the magnificent north-facing facade of its grand portico, sometimes called the "Grand Hypostyle Hall." A winged solar disk at the very top of the entrance protects the temple.

The emperor Tiberius added the portico to the temple during the first century CE. It is a massive room, about the size of two tennis courts (138 × 56 feet), and around 56 feet high. It contains twenty-four columns representing the hours of the day—twelve to the east of the central axis and twelve to the west. The six frontal columns are integrated into the façade. The other eighteen columns are within the pronaos—an architectural term to denote the inner area of the portico.

The naos-sistrum is a musical rattle that was used in ceremonial rituals associated with the goddess Hathor. It consists of a handle attached to the head of the goddess. On top of the head, there is an enclosure resembling a shrine, "the naos," where the rattle resides.

The columns in the pronaos represent gigantic, colorful sistra, and the capital of each one displays four giant Hathor faces, representing the four cardinal points. She wears a wig and has bovine ears, a reminder that she is a cow deity. Sadly, most of the goddess's gracious faces were chiseled out in ancient times by Christian iconoclasts.

The stunning decoration of the ceiling was completed during the reign of the emperor Claudius. As you enter the pronaos and look upward, you are welcomed by the magnificent scenes on the ceiling that is supported by the twenty-four columns. Three panels on each side depict the sky in vibrant colors. The walls are covered with scenes of kings giving offerings to the goddess, protective hymns, and descriptions of the New Year Festival and the Festival of Drunkenness. There is also a wall that reminds the priests how they are expected to behave when inside the hallowed temple grounds.

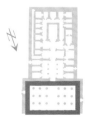

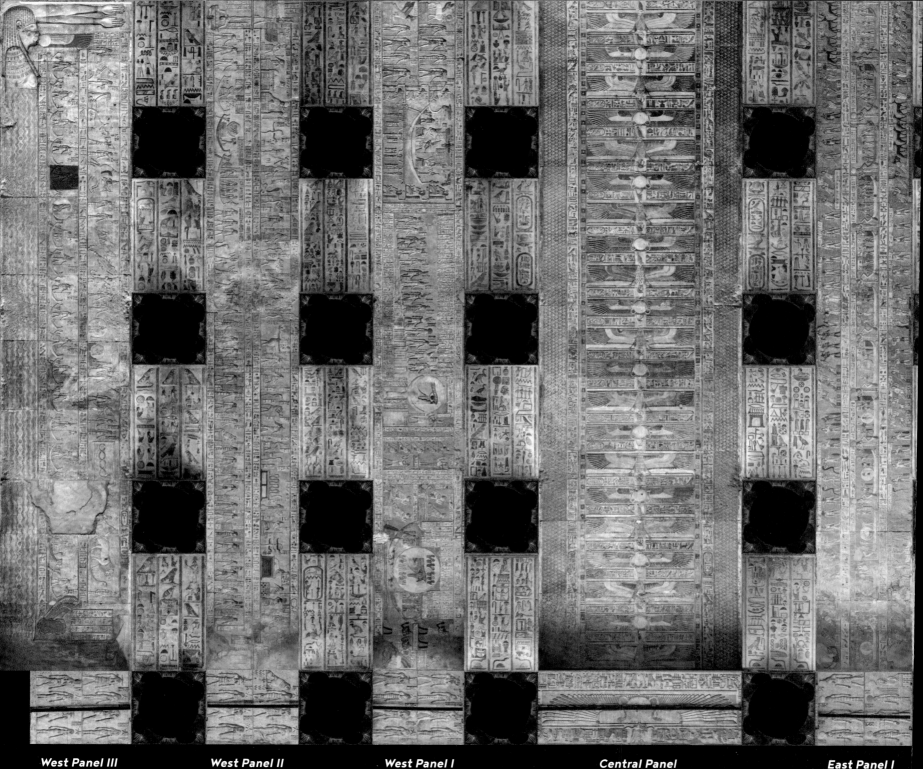

West Panel III   West Panel II   West Panel I   Central Panel   East Panel I

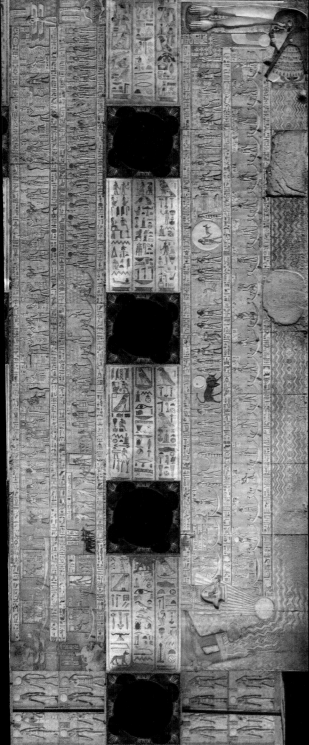

The Ceiling of the Pronaos

The ceiling of the pronaos consists of seven colored bas-relief sandstone panels—a central panel along the main corridor and three panels on either side.

The soffits of the six axial beams that support the ceiling are engraved with texts praising the Roman Emperors Caligula and Claudius, who were in power when the ceiling was decorated. The texts also honor the temple's pantheon: Horus of Edfu, Hathor, Osiris, Isis, and their children Harpocrates, Harsomtus, Ihy, and Harsesis.

The Dendera temple is oriented from north to south. The image of the ceiling presented in this composition is taken from the floor looking upward. If you stand at the entrance of the pronaos, facing north toward the Nile with the temple behind you, and hold this book over your head, you will see that the image corresponds to the ceiling above. This is why the east and the west seem to be inverted.

The ceiling is a map of time containing the majority of ancient Egyptian astronomical knowledge. It is the study of temporal properties, which include cycles and polarity.

The three panels to the east of the central panel, where the sun rises, represent day, light, and life. The three to the west, where the sun sets, represent night, darkness, and death. The "day gods" have a solar disk over their head (a circle, usually red), and the "night gods" typically have a star over their head.

2 meters

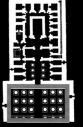

The ceiling is a rectangular coil whose central axis represents the present. Moving away from the axis, the side panels represent longer and longer cycles of duration until they reach the ceiling's edges, which represent eternity. The totality of existence is contained between the limits of the temporal frequency, which are the present and eternity.

In the central panel is the shortest possible cycle, the present. Every instant dies and becomes the past, giving way to future moments born out of the present. The past is death, absolute order, immovable and stable. It is the foundation and legacy on which the future is built: life, chaos, uncertainty, the cradle of possibilities. The present is consciousness perceiving the flow of time.

The present for the Egyptians was the pharaonic reality. The panel is an ode to the pharaoh, the supreme pontiff, who bridged the mundane and the divine. He was the incarnate god whose body was Egypt. The two lands, Upper and Lower Egypt, were unified in divine harmony under the pharaoh's authority. The lives and sweat of the Egyptians were distilled into the construction of the temples. They represented the pharaonic institution in charge of preserving harmony and imparting order under the divine authority of the pharaoh, who was Horus incarnated in life, and Osiris after his death.

The shortest cycle of time measured by the Egyptians is presented on the first panel, east from the center (East Panel I). It shows the twelve hours of the diurnal voyage of the sun, Re, over the sky. Its rise and decline are beautifully depicted as the stages of life: birth on the horizon at dawn, morning as youth and maturation, apogee at noon, serenity in the afternoon, the sunset in old age, and the culmination in the setting of the sun on the horizon to give way to the night.

The next panel, the first panel to the west of the central panel (West Panel I), shows the next cycle, the progression of days during the lunar month. The moon is predominantly nocturnal and linked with Osiris, god of the underworld. The waning and waxing moon represented his death and resurrection in his eternal struggle with darkness. When visible, the moon is the brightest object of the night. However, it also has a diurnal aspect since it may be observed during the day. This cycle of lunar phases starts with the new moon and gains one new piece every day. On the fifteenth day of the lunar month, its body is completed in the full moon, and for the next fourteen days, it loses a part until it disappears at the end of the month.

The lateral middle panels (East Panel II and West Panel II) are the transition between the day, the month, and the year. They contain the thirty-six decans, which were groups of stars used to measure the hours of the night. The decans also served to measure the passage of the year and its twelve solar months since they slowly advance in the celestial dome throughout the year (one decan every ten days).

The panels at the edges of the ceiling (East Panel III and West Panel III) show the longest cycles, the border between the year and eternity. Each of these panels is composed of two bands. The inner bands again contain the decans while the outer bands contain the constellations of the zodiac. The decans used to measure the solar year create the transition to the Great Year. The zodiac constellations pass gradually throughout the solar year. They are also the markers of the Great Year since they are slightly delayed each solar year, thus allowing the cycle of equinoctial precession to be measured.

The ceiling is framed on each side by the goddess Nut (conflated with Hathor), whose outstretched body represents heaven and earth, immovable and stable—eternity. She is the land where the Nile River flows, and she is the sky where the stars in their celestial boats sail. Her vulva and mouth are the horizons where the heavenly bodies rise and set, transitioning between day and night. The goddess Hathor is the grand theater where the cycles of existence are played out, where one is born, and the drama of death takes place.

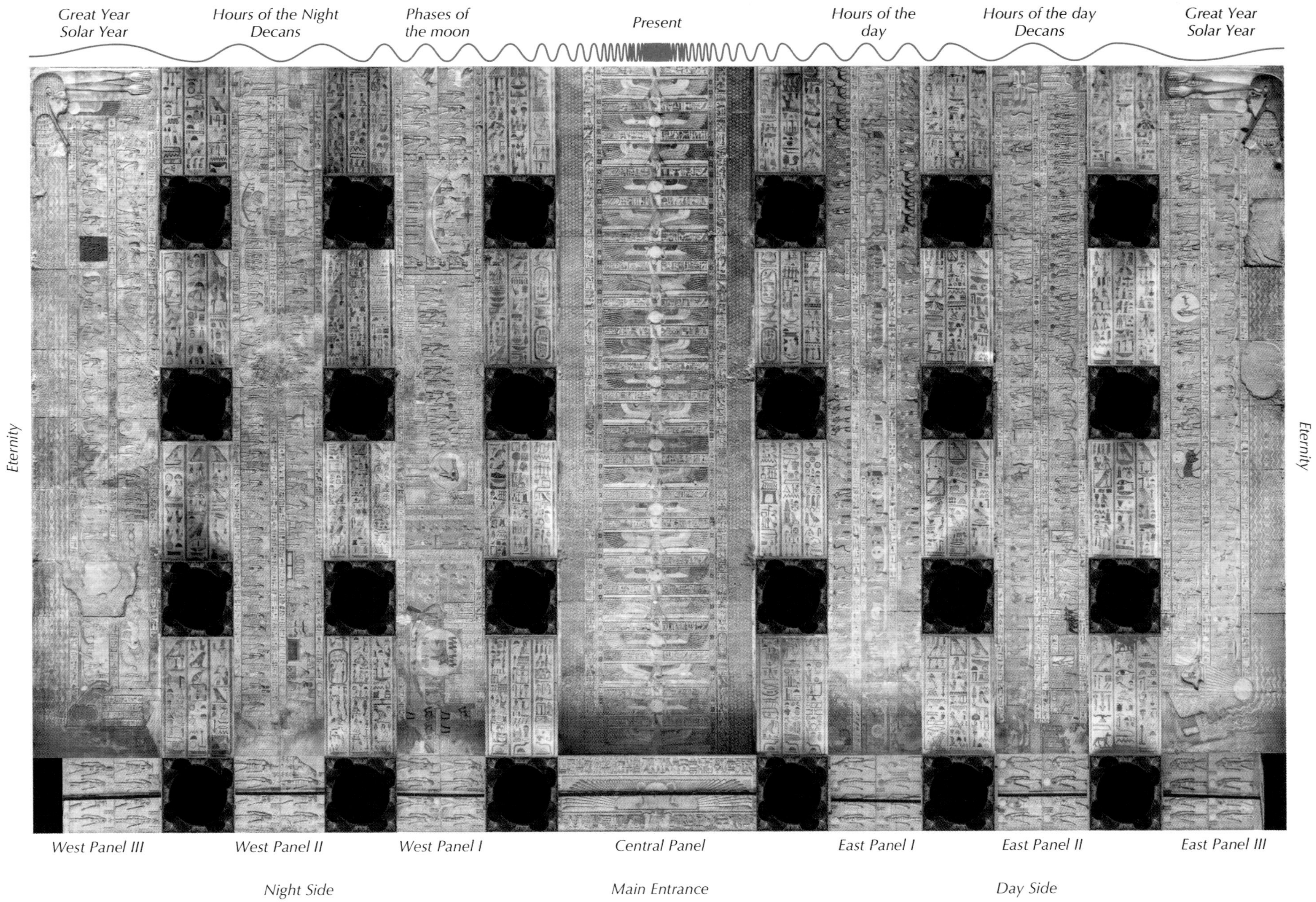

Great Year
Solar Year — Hours of the Night Decans — Phases of the moon — Present — Hours of the day — Hours of the day Decans — Great Year Solar Year

Eternity

Eternity

West Panel III — West Panel II — West Panel I — Central Panel — East Panel I — East Panel II — East Panel III

Night Side — Main Entrance — Day Side

Temporal organization of the ceiling of the pronaos.

The Central Panel

As you enter the main entrance of the pronaos and look upward, you will see the axial, central panel that directs you to the temple's inner chambers. It displays a series of winged solar disks and vultures, some of them with a cobra head (uraeus).

Egyptian pharaohs were the physical embodiment of Horus, inhabiting the earth as the sons of gods. When they died, they took the form of Osiris. The panel represents the present, the union between the mundane and the celestial. It is the link between human reality and the world of the gods.

The winged sun disks are Horus and the pharaoh. The inscriptions on the panel are dedicated to Caligula (Gaius Caesar Germanicus), the ruling emperor at the time of completion of the ceiling.

Nekhbet, the vulture goddess, was the patron of Nekhen, the ancient capital of Upper Egypt. She wears the *hedjet,* the white crown ⚪, a symbol of Upper Egypt.

Wadjet, the vulture goddess with a cobra head, was the patron of Buto, the ancient capital of Lower Egypt. She wears the red crown called the *deshret* ⚪.

Nekhbet and Wadjet accompany and protect the winged disk, which wears the double crown *pschent* ⚪, representing the union of Upper and Lower Egypt. In their claws, the birds hold the *shen* ⚪, a symbol of eternity and protection.

One of the epithets for the pharaoh was "He of the Two Ladies," referring to Nekhbet and Wadjet.

Nekhbet, a winged solar disk,
and Wadjet (top to bottom).

East Panel I

This panel is composed of three tracks. The central track portrays twelve boats used by the sun to navigate the sky in its diurnal journey from the eastern to the western horizon. Goddesses wearing solar disks over their heads facing backward stand in front of each of the boats; they are the goddesses of the hours. Groups of gods are depicted on the outer tracks, accompanying the sun and safeguarding it during its daily journey.

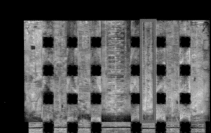

7th Hour　　　　**8th Hour**　　　　**9th Hour**　　　　**10th Hour**　　　　**11th Hour**　　　　**12th Hour**

The Diurnal Journey of Re

Re was the deity of the sun, and evidently his importance was supreme in the desert land of Egypt, where his rays burned throughout the year. But even this mighty power has cycles, and his strength is born at dawn, peaks at noon, wanes during the afternoon, and dies at nightfall.

The Egyptians imagined that the sky was an ocean where the sun sailed during the day. The solar boat of the morning was called *matet,* which means "becoming stronger." The sun navigated during the evening and night in another boat called *semket,* which means "becoming weaker." Together the two boats represented balance and order and were called *maaty* (from Maat, the principle of universal order).

The sun's diurnal journey began with its birth in the east and ended with its death when it set in the west. Hence the east was related to life and the west to death. That's why burial places in Egypt are usually located on the western bank of the Nile. The goddess associated with the entrance to the underworld was called Imentet, which means "she from the west." She wore the hieroglyph of the west over her head ⸗.

During his daily journey, Re had to deal with the forces of chaos. The sun was accompanied by protector gods in his boat who helped him in the fight with spears.

The Egyptians saw the early morning sun as the scarab Khepri, a symbol of regeneration. During the morning, the sun was Horus the child, Harpocrates, son of Osiris and Isis, and sign of the legitimate succession of the pharaohs and the morning sun.

At noon, at the sixth hour, when the sun was at its peak, Harpocrates grew to become the mighty Horus of Edfu, warrior god and avenger of his father. He was responsible for maintaining order in the universe against the forces of chaos. His symbol, the winged solar disk, became a sign of strength and protection.

During the afternoon, Re's power declined as the world began to sink into darkness. The sun was seen in the form of old Atum, who finally died at nightfall. After he descended below the horizon (*akhet*), he began his nocturnal journey through the underworld and was resurrected the next day in the form of Khepri, thereby starting a new cycle.

Thoth worships the sun at noon, its most potent time in the day. The sun is shown as a four-headed ram wearing the wadjet crown. The four heads represent the cardinal points illuminated by the sun.

Egyptians divided the daytime into twelve hours, from dawn to dusk, and divided the night in the same way. Owing to Egypt's northern latitude (between 26 and 30 degrees), daytime length varies as much as four hours during the year. Contrary to our modern horological system, wherein the duration of hours is fixed, ancient Egyptian hours changed in length depending on the length of the day. Their system was organic, based on daily solar events. There are controversies among Egyptologists about when the Egyptian day started and ended. Some propose that the day began at dawn and ended at dusk, while others claim it began at sunrise and ended at sunset. The iconography of the hours of the day at Dendera suggests the day started at dawn and ended at dusk. Seven of the twelve hours have inscriptions confirming that this is the case:

A child sucking his thumb sits at the prow of the boats for the first three hours. On the boat of the first hour, a child stands in the solar disk, and the accompanying inscription reads:

"Get up, Re, come into existence, Khepri, rise to the sky in your beautiful appearance bathed in the light of Shu."

Shu is one of the primordial gods; he represents air, and his light is the indirect light at dawn when the solar disk is not yet visible.

The child is now seated inside the solar disk during the second hour, symbolizing stability and permanence. This hour starts at sunrise when the solar disk becomes visible on the horizon. Its inscription reads:

"O Bright One, who shines with your uraeus, shine, illuminate, O Khepri!"

At the third hour, the sun is represented as a hieracosphinx, a falcon-headed sphinx resting on a lotus flower, symbolizing rebirth. This hour starts when the solar disk is fully visible over the horizon. Its inscription says:

"Awake in peace, Re who comes out of the fields of 'he of the two lions,' who is high in the sky with his uraeus, he shines on the horizon."

"He of the two lions" refers to Aker; the two lions called "yesterday" and "today" guarded the gates of the underworld at the horizon.

During the fourth and fifth hour, the boats depict the sun as an adolescent boy maturing into a stronger figure. Banebdjedet stands inside the solar disk of the sixth hour. He is the four-headed ram deity of Mendes, representing the sun at noon with his heads pointing to the four cardinal directions. The sixth hour ended at noon when the sun was at its highest point. The name of the hour was "the one who is vertical."

The seventh, eighth, and ninth hours are the first three hours of the afternoon. Their solar boats show different depictions of the sun as a vital adult. A mummy stands at the prow of the solar boat of the tenth hour, symbolizing death. This hour ends when the sun touches the horizon in the afternoon. The name of the hour was "the one whose form is hidden."

In the eleventh hour, the sun has adopted its form of Atum, the sun at sunset. At the boat's prow stands Wepwawet, the black jackal whose name means "opener of the ways," who guided the deceased in the underworld.

The twelfth hour of the day happened at twilight before dusk when the solar disk was no longer visible, but its indirect light still illuminated the sky. An old man stands on the boat of this hour accompanied by Atum.

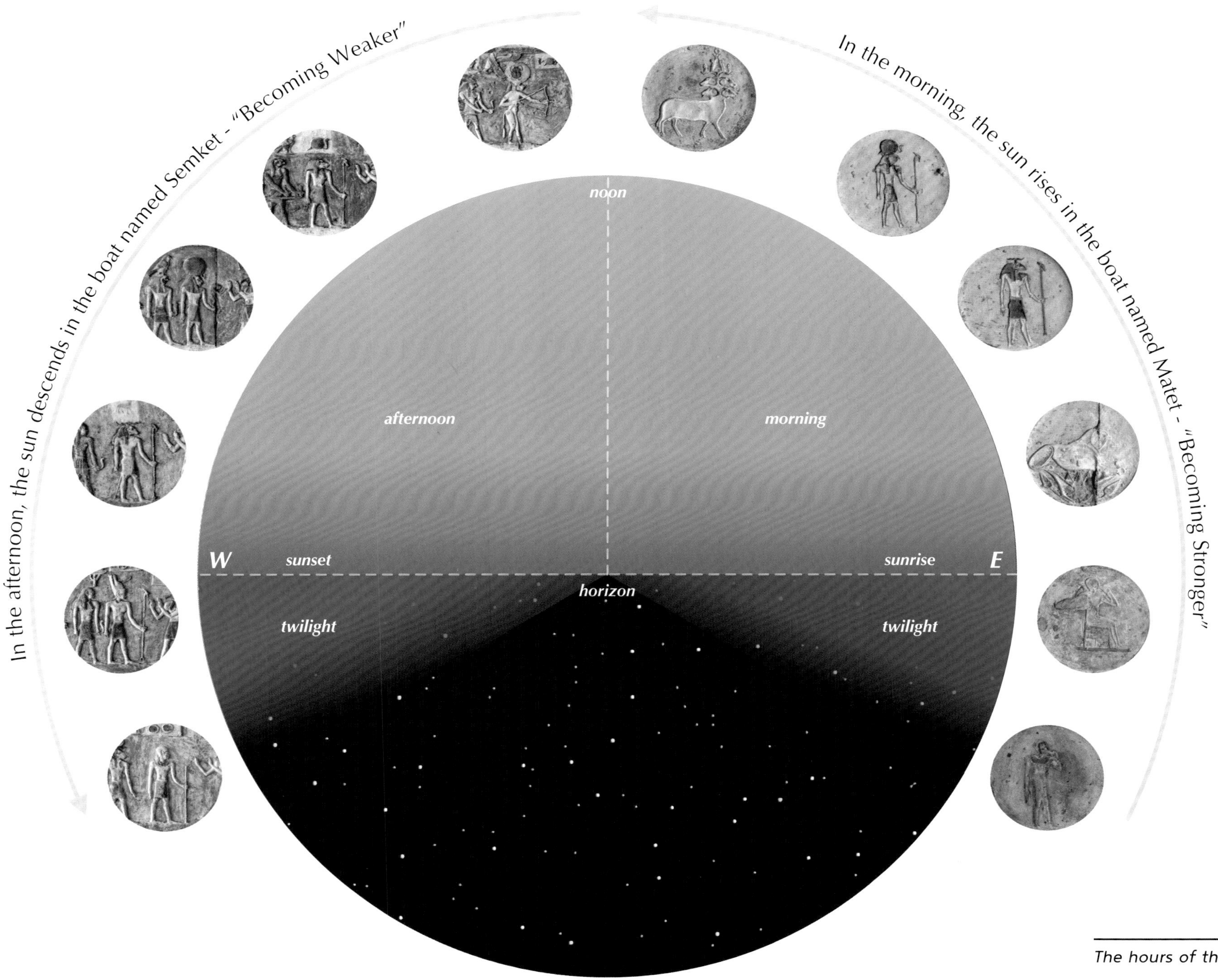

In the morning, the sun rises in the boat named Matet - "Becoming Stronger"

In the afternoon, the sun descends in the boat named Semket - "Becoming Weaker"

noon

afternoon

morning

W sunset

sunrise E

horizon

twilight

twilight

The hours of the day.

1st hour of the day

The one who illuminates

"Get up, Re, come into existence, Khepri, rise to the sky in your beautiful appearance bathed in the light of Shu."

This is the boat of the sun at dawn. A child sits at the prow, sucking his thumb. Standing behind him is Montu, killing an animal with his spear. The goddess Maat stands behind him. The newly born solar disk contains a standing child sucking his thumb. In front of him, Thoth and Isis worship him; behind, Nephthys worships as well. Montu navigates the boat at the helm.

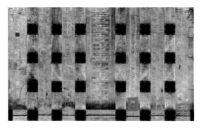

2nd hour of the day

The one who guards

"O Bright One, who shines with your uraeus, shine, illuminate, O Khepri!"

A child sits at the prow, sucking his thumb. Nefertem (god of the lotus blossom, perfumes, and the first sunlight), behind him, spears a turtle. Re, as a child, sucking his thumb, sits in the solar disk. Thoth and Neith, goddess of war and weaving, worship the sun on the right. Isis and Nephthys worship as well on the left. Sopdu, a deity of the eastern frontier, drives the boat at the helm.

3rd hour of the day
The one who protects its master

"Awake in peace, Re who comes out of the fields of 'he of the two lions,' who is high in the sky with his uraeus, he shines on the horizon."

A child sits at the prow, sucking his thumb. A ram-headed deity spearing a turtle stands behind him. Inside the solar disk, there is a lotus flower, a symbol of rebirth and renewal. A falcon-headed sphinx (hieracosphinx) lies within the flower. Thoth and Hatmehyt (a minor goddess of the city of Mendes, depicted with a fish over her head) worship the sun. The god Montu steers the boat.

4th hour of the day

The one who is hidden

"O the Brilliant One who shines with his uraeus in joy, who sails north in his time, who sails south in his time!"

A human-headed bird (representing the soul, or "ba," of Re) stands at the boat's prow. Behind him is Montu, spearing a bound man. The solar disk contains a ram-headed young god (symbolizing potency) holding a *was* scepter. Bastet (a cat-headed goddess known as "the cat of Re" who protected him against Apophis, the serpent of the underworld) and Thoth worship the sun. On the back at the helm, a falcon-headed deity steers the boat.

5th hour of the day

The one that burns

*"Re, master of the gods, appears.
He opens the secret caves."*

A bull, a symbol of virility, stands at the boat's prow. Behind it, Montu is spearing a turtle. Re stands inside the solar disk. Thoth, on the right of the disk, and Bastet and Isis, on the left, stand in worship. A man steers the boat at the helm.

6th hour of the day

The one who is vertical

"Hail to you, Khepri, who comes into existence on your own, who makes the sky and creates the earth, which founds eternity and makes infinity."

The god Tutu, a human-headed standing sphinx, protects the boat at the prow. Thoth and Bastet venerate the sun at noon. Inside the solar disk is a four-headed ram, shining in full strength in the four cardinal directions. A falcon-headed man steers at the helm.

7th hour of the day

The one who punishes

"Re appears, Power of the sky with the Unique and Splendid, arisen from Nut, the master of the appearance in the tabernacle."

Montu stands at the prow of the boat. Behind him stands Atum. The afternoon has begun, the sun starts to decline, and Re is no longer shown inside a solar disk. Protected by a vulture, Re is now a baboon-headed monkey holding a bow and arrow, crowned with a solar disk with Khepri inside. Thoth worships him while Horus commands the boat at the helm.

8th hour of the day
The one who exists

"Re appears, he wins his throne,
he sees his crown, he rules the whole country
thanks to it."

A child sits at the boat's prow with two fingers on his lips. Behind him is Horus, killing an enemy with his spear. Bastet and Thoth worship Re, depicted as an animal-headed man holding a *was* scepter and an ankh at the prime of his life. Behind him, Horus is at the helm. Note that Horus is represented twice on the boat, showing how these figures were symbolic devices, not actual beings.

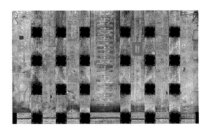

9th hour of the day

The one whose image is splendid

"Hail to you, grain god, who opens,
who is preserved, who appears, who grows,
who is renewed and rejuvenated."

A baboon sits at the boat's prow while Horus, wearing the double crown, spears an enemy. Thoth, Bastet, and Shesmetet (a protective goddess related to Bastet) worship the sun. Re is depicted as a man with a lion's head crowned with the solar disk and the uraeus. He holds an ankh in one hand and a standing baboon in the other. Horus is at the helm.

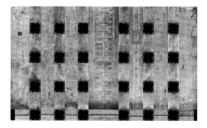

10th hour of the day

The one whose form is hidden

"Hail to you, those gods, the ancestors."

A mummy stands at the boat's prow while a donkey, a symbol of Seth, is being speared by a ram-headed god. Thoth and Maat worship Re, depicted as another ram-headed figure holding a *was* scepter. A man steers the boat.

11th hour of the day
The one whose manifestation is healthy

"The doors of the sky of Re open,
the sanctuaries of the country of Atum open."

Wepwawet, commonly mistaken for Anubis, was a black jackal known as "the opener of the ways" who guided the deceased into the underworld. He stands at the prow of the boat. Thoth, Bastet, and Hu worship the sun. Hu is the first word uttered into being by Atum at the moment of creation. He has a tongue over his head. The sun is shown in his form of Atum, pre- and post-existence, the twilight before dusk. Hu is shown again at the boat's helm.

12th hour of the day
The one that is provided with life

*"Hail to you who appeared on the horizon.
The gods come for you from heaven in worship."*

Montu stands at the prow of the boat. The sun is now an old man using a cane. Atum is behind as a ram-headed man crowned with a solar disk. Thoth and Wadjet, wearing the white crown of Upper Egypt, are worshiping the sun. Sopdu, the lord of the east, steers the boat.

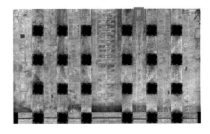

East Panel I (upper track)

4 bird-souls with baboon heads
The Souls of the East, who worship in the morning of each day.

4 standing baboons
The Souls of Jubilation, who worship Re in the east of the sky.

3 gods with jackal heads
The Providers, who are next to the rays of the solar disk.

3 baboon-headed mummies
Those pertaining to the thrones [. . .].

3 ibis-headed gods
The Gesepetiu, who pull the boat.

3 standing gods
The Referrers in the night.

3 human-headed bird-souls
The Souls of the festival of the sixth lunar month.

The upper track above the boats contains fourteen groups of deities who protected the sun god Re during his journey over the twelve hours of daylight. The track opens with the winged scarab Khepri, signaling perhaps the beginning of a new day and the rebirth of the sun. The translation to English of this track comes from the French and German of Cauville (2013a, 11) and Mendel (2022, 309-12).

3 limbed snakes

The Transporters, who push
the boat in the sky.

4 gods holding oars

The Rowers.

3 snake-headed bird-souls

The Souls of fishes and birds that cast
magical power.

3 jackal-headed gods

The Souls of Hierakonpolis.

4 jackal-headed gods

The Unwearying Ones (stars around
the celestial equator).

4 crouching lion-headed gods

The Haulers, who seize the rope in
the necropolis.

4 jackals

The Souls of the West, who
lead Re back to the shore in
the west.

East Panel I (lower track)

4 falcon-headed bird-souls
The Souls of Jubilation, who magnify things; they emerge from the day boat.

4 praising baboons
The Souls of the East, who acclaim his ka; it is they who adore Re.

3 standing gods
Those who pull the boat across the sky to the rhythm of the days.

3 baboon-headed gods
Those who belong to the place where the boat rises.

3 ram-headed gods
The Bringers, who observe the rules.

3 ibis-headed standing gods
Those who sanctify the quarters of the moon.

A bird-soul and 3 jackal bird-souls
The Souls of Neomenia (the time of the new moon).

The lower track below the boats contains fourteen groups of deities who protected the sun god Re during his journey over the twelve hours of daylight. The beginning of the track is damaged; only the tip of a pair of wings is visible. The translation to English of this track comes from the French and German of Cauville (2013a, 17) and Mendel (2022, 295-99).

3 limbed snakes
The Receivers, who utter commands to the day boat.

4 gods holding oars
The Rowers.

4 bird-souls with human heads
The Reunited Souls, who listen to the prayers and do justice for the multitude.

3 falcon-headed gods
The Souls of Pe (Buto).

4 jackals
The Indestructibles, the boat's crew (circumpolar stars).

4 crouching gods
The Figures of the night, the awakened ones who draw Re.

4 bird-souls with jackal heads
The Souls of the West, who receive Re in peace.

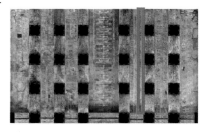

West Panel I

The first panel to the west of the central corridor is devoted to the moon. It is subdivided into four distinct scenes. There is a debate among scholars about the precise interpretation of the four scenes on this panel. I have used the interpretation presented by Dr. Gyula Priskin, who claims that the first panel (from the right) represents the waning phase of the moon. The second one, much narrower than the others, shows the new moon. The third one is the waxing phase, and the last one is the full moon.

The moon is a tragic character whose body loses a piece each day during its waning phase until it disappears as the new moon and is reconstituted in its waxing phase until it reaches fullness as the full moon. It is the only celestial body whose

The moon is Osiris, a mysterious and liminal being, ruler of the night but also present during the day. He was the husband and brother of Isis and was known for being murdered and dismembered into fourteen parts by his brother Seth. Isis recovered all the parts except the phallus. She made a golden replica to take its place and used her magic to reconstitute and reanimate the body of Osiris with whom she then conceived their son Horus.

The sun penetrates the darkness of the night, reflecting its light over the moon. Osiris is the seed that fecundates Isis to conceive the new sun, Horus, who will be nourished in the womb of Hathor with her milk, the Milky Way. Hathor—*het-her*—literally means "the house of Horus," which is interpreted as "the womb

The New Moon   *The Waning of the Moon*

Plutarch relates the relationship between the moon, Isis, and Osiris:

> *Thus they make the power of Osiris to be fixed in the moon, and say that Isis, since she is generation, is associated with him. For this reason they also call the moon the mother of the world, and they think that she has a nature both male and female, as she is receptive and made pregnant by the Sun, but she herself in turn emits and disseminates into the air generative principles. For, as they believe, the destructive activity of Typhon [Seth] does not always prevail, but oftentimes is overpowered by such generation and put in bonds, and then at a later time is again released and contends against Horus, who is the terrestrial universe; and this is never completely exempt either from dissolution or from generation. (Plutarch tr. 1927)*

Isis is generation, and her twin sister Nephthys is dissolution. Together they are the two inseparable faces of life's coin.

Fertility and the Moon

Ancient Egyptians divided the year into three seasons: flood, cultivation, and harvest. The flood was the beginning of the annual fertility cycle of the land.

They believed that the Nile's flooding was due to the tears shed by Isis after the death of her beloved Osiris. The star Sirius, personified by Isis, marked the beginning of the flood.

The French Egyptologist Gaston Maspero, who observed the flooding of the Nile in the eighteenth century before it was dammed, stated:

> As the successive floods grow stronger and are more heavily charged with mud, the whole mass of water becomes turbid and changes colour. In eight or ten days it has turned from greyish blue to dark red, occasionally of so intense a color as to look like newly shed blood. (Maspero 1894)

Once the waters receded, the fertile and moist banks of the Nile were ready for planting. The mummified body of Osiris, in his form of Osiris-Neper, is the seed that, after being buried, resurrects in the form of a seedling, thus beginning a new life cycle.

Plutarch described the roles of Osiris and Isis:

> As they regard the Nile as the effusion of Osiris, so they hold and believe the earth to be the body of Isis, not all of it, but so much of it as the Nile covers, fertilizing it and uniting with it. (Plutarch tr. 1927)

The Osiris myth in which the goddess Isis reconstitutes the body of her beloved after it was dismembered by Seth into fourteen parts is also an allegory of the lunar phases.

Observing those phases, Egyptians learned to measure the lunar cycle. That is why Osiris is the one who teaches humans to cultivate, since the month is the measure of the rhythm of fertility—menstruation. The words *menstruation, commensurate, month,* and *moon* all come from the same root meaning "to measure."

The Egyptians had no way of knowing about the existence of the ova. For them, the womb was analogous to the black earth on the riverbanks after the flood.

Menstrual bleeding is the flood that marks the beginning of the female fertility cycle. Fourteen days later, the uterine soil is ripe to be impregnated by the male seed—Osiris.

In the scene of the full moon, Khepri, the new sun, stands in the balance between Isis and Nephthys. If the fertilization is successful, the generative forces of Isis will prevail, and a new pregnancy will start. If not, Nephthys—dissolution—will take over, and the bleeding will come again, beginning a new cycle.

In my opinion, it is not far-fetched to see how the Osiris myth could be used as a magic formula to calculate the rhythms of human fertility and conception.

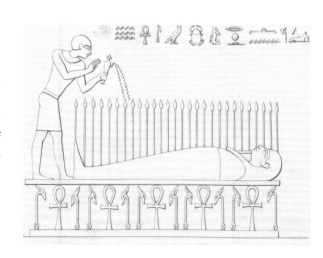

Osiris-Neper, with twenty-eight stalks of wheat growing from his body. Bas-relief at Philae. Illustration by Giuseppe Angelelli.

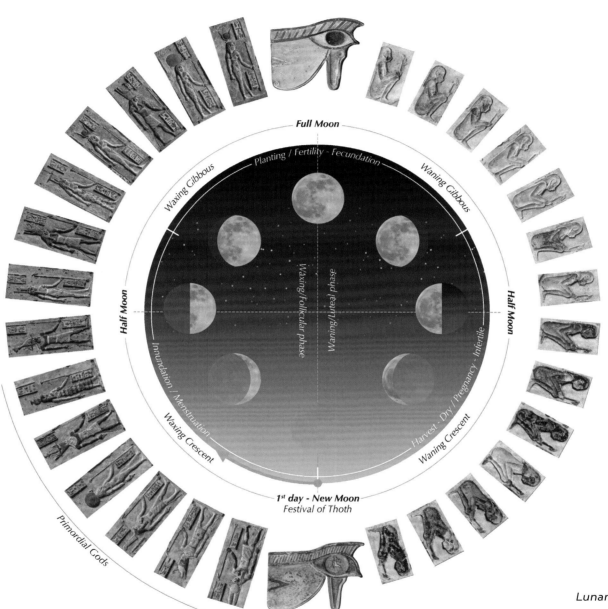

Lunar month, phases of the moon,
and menstrual cycle.

The Waning of the Moon

The Osirian boat carries the moon disk. Fourteen crouched Sethian deities hold the *was* scepter, surrounding the eye. They remove a slice of the moon every day of the waning phase. The lower seven have a light color, symbolizing the waning gibbous, and the other seven are dark, representing the waning crescent. These deities surround the *wedjat* eye, at the last stage of the phase: the new moon. The eye's sclera is black since no light shines on the moon at that time. In the pupil is Horus the Child, the seed of the new sun.

Osiris is accompanied in his boat by Thoth, Isis, and Horus. Horus Khenty-khety ("foremost retreater") steers at the helm. He is a god usually represented as a man with the head of a falcon, carrying in his hands the two eyes that represent the sun and the moon.

Above the boat, the text reads (translation from Cauville's French):

> *You appear, you shine, Osiris in the Sky, you shine in the horizon of the sky. . . . Osiris, the Great God, the Regent of eternity, presides over the west under the form of a 'victor.' Heaven is in joy containing your mysterious image. The left eye meets the right eye; the time of the moon has come. There is no irregularity in all your ritual from morning to night. (Cauville 2013a, 39)*

The boat is surrounded by four jackals, guardian souls of the night, and four human-headed birds whose inscription reads:

> *The Souls of Egypt transfigure the* wedjat *eye, he who renews his cycle on the fifteenth day, they escort the god in his form of a venerable child, providing for him the* wedjat *eye with its perfect elements. (Cauville 2013a, 39)*

Behind the jackals stands the Wind of the East, who has the body of a bird (his head is damaged). Below is the Wind of the North, represented as a winged ram.

Contrary to Priskin, Cauville considers that this scene represents the moon in gestation and that the fourteen gods around the eye are fetuses of the deities that will be revealed each day of the waxing of the moon. (Cauville 2013b, 513)

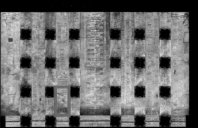

The New Moon

This is one of the most cryptic scenes in the whole ceiling. It contains Isis and Thoth worshiping five falcons. The text surrounding the hawks explains that they are Horus and his four children.

The sons of Horus were the personifications of the canopic jars used to store different human organs during mummification. Their names were Imsety, Duamutef, Hapi, and Qebehsenuef. They contained the liver, stomach, lungs, and intestines, respectively. Each of them also represented one of the cardinal directions.

According to Gyula Priskin, this panel represents the new moon:

> *The second scene from the right, that of Isis and Thoth adoring the five falcons, is unquestionably linked to the invisibility of the moon, since at the beginning of the relevant text a clear reference is made to the new moon in the third month of the Shemu season, when Osiris is said to come to see Isis. . . . This is also the time, as was suggested earlier, when traditionally Hathor of Dendera visited her spouse, Horus, in Edfu as part of the beautiful reunion of the two divine beings. (Priskin 2016, 133)*

Priskin also notes that the number five is a cryptological reference to the three days of invisibility of the moon (which is the fifth part of a half lunar month, $15 \div 5 = 3$) as stated in a spell of the Coffin Texts (a collection of funerary protective spells written on Middle Kingdom coffins to aid the deceased in dealing with the dangers encountered in the underworld).

Mendel theorizes that this section of the lunar panel represents a formula for converting oipes into Persian artabas, which were units used by the ancient Egyptians to measure grains (Mendel 2022, 269).

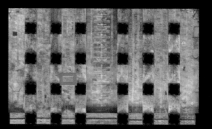

The Waxing of the Moon

Seth, Osiris's brother, is the shadow who dismembers his brother into fourteen parts during the waning phase of the moon.

The third scene of the panel represents the waxing phase of the moon. The gestation period from the new moon to the full moon is when Osiris successfully conquers darkness. This scene is a temporal diagram to be read from right to left.

The Egyptian lunar month began with the new moon when the festival of Thoth was celebrated. He presides over the scene.

As the waxing progresses, the gods of the Ennead (the main deities of the Egyptian pantheon, more information on p. 64) contribute to the reconstitution of the lunar disc.

The primordial gods on the upper steps of the stairway walking toward the moon represent the waxing crescent, as they are the first to reach the lunar disk. They are (from right to left) Montu, Atum, Shu, Tefnut, Geb, and Nut.

Contributing to the waxing gibbous are Osiris (after Nut, continuing from right to left), Isis, Horus son of Isis, Nephthys, Hathor, Horus of Edfu, Tanenet, and Iunit.

All deities climbing the stairs hold the ankh and a scepter. Male gods hold the *was* scepter, a Sethian symbol. The act of holding it represents control and power over chaos. Female deities hold the *wadj* scepter, which is papyrus-tipped, and represents health and vitality.

The lunar disk reflecting the solar light in the form of an eye is depicted as a mirror with a handle in the shape of a papyrus column—an object associated with the goddess Hathor.

The names of the days of the lunar month and their corresponding festivals are inscribed on the vertical hieroglyphic columns underneath the stairway.

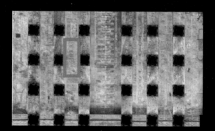

The Eye of Horus

Numerous myths describe the adventures of Re's eyes.

Isis, aspiring to gain Re's magical powers, poisons him with a snake bite, and in exchange for the cure, Re gives her his eyes. Isis gives the eyes to her son Horus, who then takes Re's place.

In a battle with Seth, Horus loses one of Re's eyes, and Seth destroys it. The god Thoth performs magic to reconstruct the destroyed eye, and Horus gives it to his father Osiris, who then uses it to achieve eternal life in the underworld.

The eyes of Horus are the two most prominent celestial objects. The right eye represents the sun and the left, the moon. Owing to the damage done by Seth, the left eye, the moon, is fainter than the other. The sun is the regent of the day, and the moon is the nocturnal substitute for the sun, which explains the lunar association of Osiris, lord of the night. The moon, a symbol of fertility, was associated with the bovine, its horns symbolizing the crescent moon (more information on p. 130).

The eye of Horus was known as the *wedjat,* meaning "complete," or "sound one." The symbol of the *wedjat* proliferated in ancient Egypt, often appearing as an amulet placed with diseased bodies for protection in the afterlife.

In the central lunar scene of the pronaos, representing the waxing moon, Thoth presides over the reconstruction of the left eye of Horus with the help of the fourteen gods ascending a staircase toward the eye. The reconstructed eye, which represents the full moon, is the body of Osiris that Seth cut into fourteen pieces. The gods who participate in the reconstruction of the eye, the Ennead, represent the fundamental aspects of the creation process.

The Heliopolitan Ennead

At face value, the proliferation of deities in Egyptian mythology is astonishing. But the reality is that Egyptian gods were embodiments of natural properties. Once this is understood, many of the strange contradictions and paradoxes posed by the myths go away.

For example, depending on its stage in the sky during the day, the sun is seen as different manifestations of Re: Khepri is the sun at dawn, Horus the child is the sun at sunrise, Horus of Edfu is the sun at noon, and Atum the sun in the evening.

Another complication is that many deities either gained or declined in popularity during the extended history of ancient Egypt. Part of the explanation is that as various political centers became ascendant, their local deities gained importance and absorbed the attributes of the less fortunate.

Hathor, for example, has many faces: Nut-Hathor (the sky), Hathor-Isis, Isis-Hathor-Sothis, and Hathor-Sekhmet.

The traditional Heliopolitan Ennead (the main deities worshiped at Heliopolis) is composed of nine deities (hence the name, from "nine"): Atum, Shu, Tefnut, Geb, Nut, Osiris, Isis, Seth, and Nephthys. These are the deities who take part in creation.

The extended Ennead shown in the scene of the waxing moon includes six more gods. Part of the reason seems political and part is simply to contribute the additional number of days necessary to complete the moon's waxing. The additional gods are Montu (Upper Egypt's counterpart of Atum), Iunit and Tanenet (consorts of Montu), Horus son of Isis, Horus of Edfu, and Thoth. Seth is excluded from the scene. Seen as evil in late Egypt, he mostly vanished from Ptolemaic temples, except when being harpooned or punished. In the staircase of the waxing moon scene, his rightful place is taken by Horus son of Isis, when in reality he, and not Horus, is the husband of Nephthys.

Atum is the self-created origin of all things. He is the monad. Shu and Tefnut represent duality, which is a requisite for existence. Geb and Nut are the earth and sky, matter and space, required for material existence. Their progeny, Osiris, Seth, Isis, and Nephthys, are the first cyclical temporal aspects of reality and opposite forces: creation, destruction, generation, and dissolution. Horus is life incarnated, the quintessence. Hathor is the womb of creation, the theater of existence.

Thoth is the artificer, the master of language, capable of discerning good from evil and order from chaos. In one account he emerged from Seth's head from the seed of Horus. In another he is self-generated.

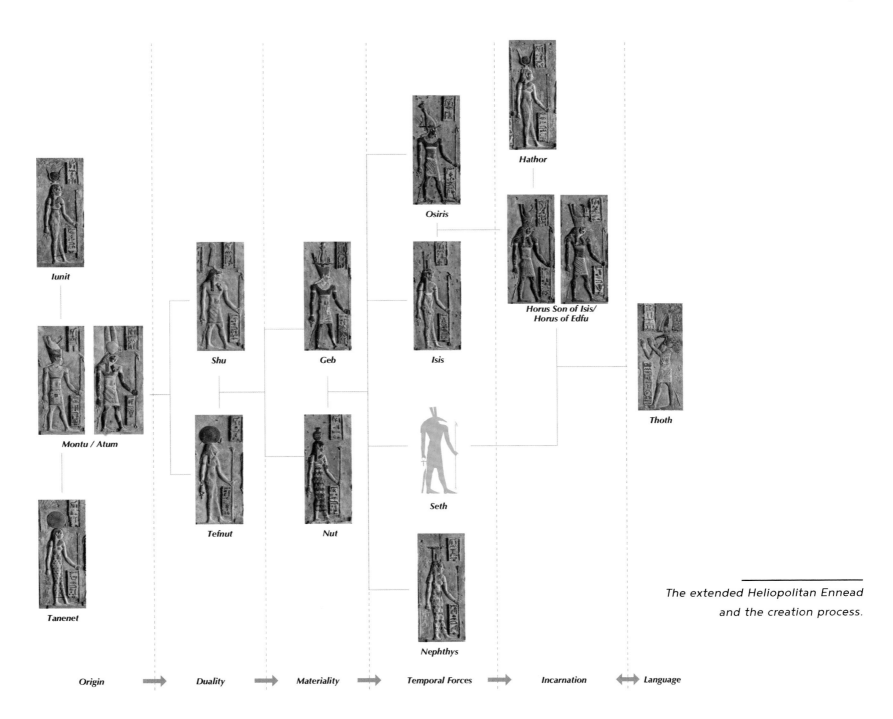

Iunit

Montu / Atum

Tanenet

Shu

Tefnut

Geb

Nut

Osiris

Isis

Seth

Nephthys

Hathor

Horus Son of Isis/
Horus of Edfu

Thoth

Origin   ⟶   Duality   ⟶   Materiality   ⟶   Temporal Forces   ⟶   Incarnation   ⟷   Language

The extended Heliopolitan Ennead
and the creation process.

Thoth

Thoth, or *dhwty,* anglicized as Djehuty, and meaning "he who is like the ibis," was known as Hermes by the Greeks and as Mercury by the Romans. Thoth was the lunar god of magic, language, numbers, and wisdom.

As scribe of the gods, he is credited with the invention of writing and measurement. Thoth was the father of astronomy and was responsible for the reckoning of time and the seasons.

The origin of Thoth is contested. One version says he was self-created, the other claims that during one of the battles between Horus and Seth, they engaged in a sexual act and the product of that act was Thoth, born from the seed of Horus.

As the arbiter and settler of disputes, Thoth brought balance to the struggle between order and chaos. He was a symbol of justice and overseer of the weighing of the heart of the deceased. This ceremony took place at the time of death, when one's heart was weighed against the feather of truth, and the result would decide whether an individual could enter the afterlife.

The Egyptians portrayed him as an ibis or as an ibis-headed man, although sometimes he appears as a baboon. Thoth was the god of transitions and borders and the mediator of worlds. He was the spirit at dawn, the moment of awakening.

Here is an account of the attributes of Thoth according to Diodorus of Sicily:

The one most highly honored by him [Osiris] was Hermes, who was endowed with unusual ingenuity for devising things capable of improving the social life of man.

It was by Hermes, for instance, according to them [the Egyptians], that the common language of mankind was first further articulated, and that many objects which were still nameless received an appellation, that the alphabet was invented, and that ordinances regarding the honors and offerings due to the gods were duly established; he was the first also to observe the orderly arrangement of the stars and the harmony of the musical sounds and their nature, to establish a wrestling school, and to give thought to the rhythmical movement of the human body and its proper development. He also made a lyre and gave it three strings, imitating the seasons of the year; for he adopted three tones, a high, a low, and a medium; the high from the summer, the low from the winter, and the medium from the spring. (Diodorus tr. 1933)

As measurer of time, Thoth was also credited with creating the 365-day calendar.

Thoth's main cult center was Khemenu, a city at the boundary of Lower and Upper Egypt known by the Greeks as Hermopolis (city of Hermes).

Montu

Montu, or *mntw,* meaning "nomad," was a solar god usually portrayed as a human with a falcon's head, crowned with the solar disk with a double uraeus and two feathers. He was depicted as a sacred bull on other occasions, representing the strength and fury of a charging bull. Montu's consorts were the goddesses Iunit and Tanenet.

Montu was one of the protectors of Re during his nightly journey through the Duat. He seems to have been a personification of the destructive heat of the sun.

He is an ancient deity originally worshiped at Hermonthis. His cult spread during the Eleventh Dynasty, and he became a powerful state god of Thebes and one of the most important deities of Egypt. Montu-Re was Upper Egypt's counterpart of Atum-Re, from Lower Egypt.

Various kings adopted his name, the most illustrious being Montuhotep II, who united Upper and Lower Egypt after the First Intermediate Period. His popularity declined after the Eleventh Dynasty, and, eventually, Amun (a god associated with fertility and war, not to be confused with Atum) took his place.

Atum

Of all the ancient Egyptian divine genealogies, the most famous is the one from Heliopolis. The head of the family was the god Atum, father of two children, Shu and Tefnut. They, in turn, had two offspring, Geb and Nut, who had between them, according to different sources, either four or five children: Osiris, Horus the Elder, Isis, Seth, and Nephthys.

Ancient Egyptians conceived of the world as being created ex nihilo. Before anything existed, there was Nun, the primeval waters of chaos and darkness, the nothingness from which everything arose. Every generation of the divine family tree represented the principles involved at each step of the creation process. This cosmological myth survives in the Bremner-Rhind papyrus, which describes Atum, the creator god:

> *"I came into being in the form of Khepri when I came into being, and that is how 'Being' came into being, because I was more primaeval than the primaeval ones whom I had made; . . . After I had made excitation with my fist, my desire came into mine hand, and seed fell from my mouth; I spat out Shu and expectorated Tefnut." (Faulkner 1938)*

The name of the god Atum comes from the word *tm,* which means "completeness," "to be complete." He was the creator god of everything from the Heliopolitan Ennead. Being the primordial one, he created the first couple—Shu and Tefnut—from his seed in a masturbatory act. He is the monad and represents both pre- and post-existence.

Egyptians usually depicted Atum in human form wearing the double crown of Upper and Lower Egypt.

Atum was one of the manifestations of the sun. In particular, he was associated with the setting sun and with Khepri, the sun at dawn.

Tefnut ⌇ and Shu ⌇

Shu and Tefnut were the progeny of Atum, the creator god of the Heliopolitan Ennead. The male Shu, or *šw,* meant emptiness, as in space, or dryness, and the female Tefnut, or *tfnwt,* personified moisture. Her name comes from the verb *tfn,* meaning "to spit," as Atum spat her out at the moment of her creation. Their names are onomatopoeic, as they make the sounds of the wind and of spitting.

Shu, the cool and dry wind from the north, represented order and balance. He wears on his head the ostrich feather of Maat to convey these attributes. Shu usually holds an ankh and a *was* scepter, symbols of life and power. As the god of space and air, he maintained the separation of Geb and Nut (the sky and earth) by placing himself in between them (more about this in the chapter "Nut and Geb").

Shu's sister, Tefnut, is usually depicted as a lioness crowned with an uraeus solar disk. She holds a *wadj* scepter (tipped with a papyrus flower) in one hand and an ankh in the other. According to one account, she became a ferocious lioness who rampaged the lands of Nubia. Thoth and Shu had to follow and appease her. Some of the destructive aspects of Tefnut were incorporated into the mythology of the goddess Hathor.

As the first couple, Shu and Tefnut symbolize duality. They represented two complementary and opposite aspects: dryness and moisture, order and chaos. They are the duad that emanated from their monadic father, Atum, illustrating the essential step for creation, whereby one becomes two. Shu and Tefnut gave birth to Geb and Nut, who represent the material world. This was the primary justification for divine rulership in the Amarna period as Akhenaten and Nefertiti compared themselves to Shu and Tefnut. It was also an important way of incorporating a female aspect into the monotheistic Aten religion, further emphasizing the duality of the universe.

The main cult center of Shu and Tefnut was at Leontopolis (Greek for "city of lions") in Lower Egypt, where they were worshiped in the form of lions.

The builders of Dendera immortalized these twins on the ceiling of the pronaos as the Gemini constellation in the upper track of East Panel III.

Nut ⬚ and Geb ⬚

Geb and Nut belonged to the Heliopolitan Ennead. They were the offspring of Shu and Tefnut and the grandchildren of Atum, the primordial creator god. Geb is usually depicted in human form wearing the *shuti* crown (ram horns and two feathers). Sometimes he is shown with a goose over his head instead of the crown. His sister and consort Nut is usually depicted wearing a waterpot over her head, which is a hieroglyphic sign in her name. At other times she appears as a cow.

These twins were inseparable when they came into being, leaving no room for further creation. Their father Shu, representing air and space, had to intervene and stand between them so as to separate them. This is one of the most iconic images from ancient Egypt: Geb lying down while Nut arches on top of him. With this separation, Geb came to represent the earth and Nut the sky.

Together they had five children: Osiris, Horus the Elder, Seth, Isis, and Nephthys, which represent the five epagomenal days. Plutarch relates the story:

They [the Egyptians] say that the Sun [Re], when he became aware of Rhea's [Nut's] intercourse with Cronus [Geb], invoked a curse upon her that she should not give birth to a child in any month or any year; but Hermes, being enamoured of the goddess, consorted with her. Later, playing at draughts with the moon, he won from her the seventieth part of each of her periods of illumination, and from all the winnings he composed five days, and intercalated them as an addition to the three hundred and sixty days. The Egyptians even now call these five days intercalated and celebrate them as the birthdays of the gods. They relate that on the first of these days Osiris was born. . . . On the second of these days Arueris was born whom they call Apollo, and some call him also the elder Horus. On the third day Typhon [Seth] was born. . . . On the fourth day Isis was born in the regions that are ever moist; and on the fifth Nephthys. (Plutarch tr. 1927)

Geb and Nut were the first "tangible" manifestations of creation in Heliopolitan cosmology. Their parents, Shu and Tefnut, who are the first couple, representing duality, are the condition for their existence.

Osiris

Osiris is the Greek name for the god known to the Egyptians as *wsjr,* anglicized as Asar.

He is usually depicted as a mummy with a green face, wearing the feathered white crown called the *atef* and holding the crook and the flail crossed over his chest, symbols of kingship. The main center of worship of Osiris was in Abydos.

Osiris was the eldest son of Geb and Nut. In his coming of age, he became the king of Egypt. Osiris gave agriculture and law to his people in his role as king.

His brother Seth grew jealous and created an elaborate plan to overthrow Osiris and usurp his throne. He made a chest to the exact size of Osiris and convinced him to lie down in it. Once Osiris was inside, Seth sealed it and threw it into the Nile where it meets the sea.

When Isis found out what had happened to her husband, she looked for him throughout Egypt. She finally learned that the sea had carried the chest to the shores of Byblos, in modern-day Lebanon, where it had become trapped in the trunk of a tamarisk tree. Isis recovered the body and took it to the desert, where she used her magic to temporarily animate the body so as to conceive their son Horus.

Seth subsequently discovered the unattended body of Osiris and tore it into fourteen pieces that he scattered around Egypt. With the help of her sister Nephthys,

Isis found all the parts except for one. An Oxyrhynchus fish had eaten the phallus, which Isis replaced with a gold replica.

Isis, with the help of Anubis, then mummified Osiris. Finally, using her magic, she brought him back to life. Osiris then became the king of the underworld. Plutarch gives us an insight into the nature of Osiris:

> But the wiser of the priests call not only the Nile Osiris and the sea Typhon [Seth], but they simply give the name of Osiris to the whole source and faculty creative of moisture, believing this to be the cause of generation and the substance of life-producing seed; and the name of Typhon they give to all that is dry, fiery, and arid, in general, and antagonistic to moisture. (Plutarch tr. 1927)

At one level, the Osiris myth describes the annual cycle of inundation and withdrawal of the Nile—how the great river's waters advance into the desert, bringing fertility, and how the desert advances across the fertile land when the waters recede, bringing sterility.

As mentioned previously, Osiris gave agriculture to the Egyptians. He was the vital force of nature that made vegetation grow, participating in an eternal dance (or struggle) with Seth, his brother and counterpart, who was the personification of decay and dissolution. Together they represented the cycle of life and death.

Isis

Isis is the Greek name of the goddess *3st,* commonly anglicized as Aset. Her records go back to the Fifth Dynasty, and her origins are uncertain. Over time her popularity grew, and her worship spread throughout Greece and the Roman Empire. The Isis cult lasted until the sixth century CE, during the reign of the emperor Justinian, when her last temple, located on the island of Philae, was converted into a Christian church. As time went by, Isis acquired the attributes of other goddesses.

Isis was usually depicted as a woman with a throne over her head, reflecting a hieroglyph in her name. Oftentimes she had wings beneath her arms and held the ankh and a scepter. In later periods, she was portrayed wearing the horned solar disk of Hathor.

One of the essential magical beliefs of the Egyptians was that everyone had a secret name called the *ren* (another word for "name"). Whoever knew the *ren* of things had control over them. Isis longed to know the secret name of Re so she could gain his powers. Using her magic, Isis made a snake out of Re's saliva and had it bite him. According to Isis, the only way for Re to be healed was to give her his secret name, to which Re inevitably consented. Having acquired his powers, Isis gave the two eyes of Re to her son Horus, who became the new sun god and was amalgamated with Re.

Isis was born on the fourth epagomenal day. She was the daughter of Geb and Nut and the loyal wife of her oldest brother, Osiris. As a couple, they represent the cycles of growth, death, and renewal. She was the all-loving archetypal mother, a fertility goddess, protector of the dead, and a powerful and wise magician.

According to Plutarch:

> *Isis is, in fact, the female principle of Nature, and is receptive of every form of generation, in accord with which she is called by Plato the gentle nurse and the all-receptive, and by most people has been called by countless names, since, because of the force of Reason, she turns herself to this thing or that and is receptive of all manner of shapes and forms. (Plutarch tr. 1927)*

Apuleius, a Numidian (present-day Algeria) writer and philosopher, who seems to have been an initiate of the cult of Isis from the second century CE, describes the festivals and processions celebrated in spring and fall in honor of the goddess in his book *The Golden Ass*.

Horus, Son of Isis

Horus was the Greek name of the god known by the Egyptians as *ḥr*, commonly anglicized as Heru. He was widely worshiped throughout Egypt and was depicted as a falcon or a falcon-headed man wearing the double crown signifying the unification of Upper and Lower Egypt. He was a solar, tutelary god in charge of maintaining order against the forces of disorder, as embodied by his uncle and nemesis, Seth. Pharaohs were considered to be living incarnations of Horus.

He was the son of Isis and Osiris, conceived after his father's death.

The worship of Horus took many forms: Harpocrates (a Greek name meaning "Horus the child") is the god of silence and symbol of the sun at dawn. Horus of Edfu represents the sun at noon, at its highest force. Horus the Elder, son of Geb and Nut, is one of the oldest gods in ancient Egypt; his eyes were the sun and the moon. Horus in the Horizon is a falcon-headed sphinx and represents the early sun.

According to Diodorus of Sicily:

> *And it appears that Horus was the last of the gods to be king after his father Osiris departed from among men. Moreover, they say that the name Horus, when translated, is Apollo, and that, having been instructed by his mother Isis in both medicine and divination, he is now a benefactor of the race of men through his oracular responses and his healings. (Diodorus tr. 1933)*

Nephthys

Nephthys is the Greek name of the goddess *nbt-ḥwt,* which means "lady of the house," from *nbt* ("lady") and *ḥwt* ("house"). In the context of Nephthys's name, *ḥwt,* as in the name of Hathor (*ḥwt-ḥr* meaning "house of Horus"), can be understood as the "heaven" above the sun.

Nephthys was the daughter of Geb and Nut and the sister of Osiris, Isis, and Seth. She was the wife of Seth but had an affair with Osiris, out of which Anubis was born. She wears the hieroglyphs of her name over her head and is usually depicted with her sister Isis.

Plutarch describes the role of Nephthys in the ancient Egyptian tradition:

> The outmost parts of the land beside the mountains and bordering on the sea the Egyptians call Nephthys. This is why they give to Nephthys the name of "Finality," and say that she is the wife of Typhon [Seth]. Whenever, then, the Nile overflows and with abounding waters spreads far away to those who dwell in the outermost regions, they call this the union of Osiris with Nephthys, which is proved by the upspringing of the plants. . . . Typhon gained knowledge of the wrong done to his bed. So Isis gave birth to Horus in lawful wedlock, but Nephthys bore Anubis clandestinely. . . . Nephthys, after her marriage to Typhon, was at first barren . . . they must mean by it the utter barrenness and unproductivity of the earth resulting from a hard-baked soil. (Plutarch tr. 1927)

Nephthys represented death, decay, and dissolution in contrast to her sister, Isis, who was vitality, fertility, and growth.

Hathor

Hathor is one of the oldest known goddesses of ancient Egypt. Her name, *ḥwt-ḥr*, means "house of Horus." One way to write her name using hieroglyphs is to draw a falcon inside a house. The falcon is the prevailing symbol of Horus, her husband.

As for her image, Hathor is commonly associated with the cow. She is very often shown with the sun disk and horns on her head. Her anthropomorphic form, too, is shown with a disk and horns. When she is present in the capitals of columns, she has bovine ears and wears a wig with thick strands of hair, facing directly forward. Out of all the Egyptian deities, only she and the god Bes are depicted in a frontal view.

Her most important cult center was Dendera, although she was worshiped throughout Egypt. Her image is found in many temples, especially those consecrated to goddesses and, in particular, the so-called *mammisi* temples (*mammisi* means "birthplace") of the Ptolemaic period, dedicated to the childbirth of divine children.

Two other important temples dedicated to the goddess are located in southern Egypt: one at Philae and the other at Abu Simbel. The latter was built by Ramesses II for his wife Nefertari and was relocated in 1964 to avoid flooding after the construction of the Aswan High Dam. Hathor also appears on the beautifully illustrated walls of Nefertari's tomb in the Valley of the Queens (denominated QV66).

Hathor was a sun goddess, the counterpart of Re. In some stories, she is the daughter of Re and was born as her father's eye, alluded to by the sun disk above her head.

Over the course of her extensive history, Hathor assumed many roles, including that of a goddess of healing. According to one myth, she magically restored the wounded eye of Horus after he had battled with Seth.

Hathor was a personification of emotions, usually known as the goddess of joy, music, intoxication, and celebration. However, she also has a dark side. At one point, Hathor transforms into a lioness and descends into the world to slaughter humans, punishing them for rebelling against her father, Re. She enjoyed the carnage so much that other gods, fearing the annihilation of humanity, had to intervene and intoxicate her with beer to appease her.

Hathor was also the goddess of love, fertility, and beauty. The Greeks identified her as Aphrodite. Inside her temple at Dendera, there is a relief of Hathor, crouched while giving birth, as one of her functions was to assist women in childbirth.

Hathor was also a celestial goddess for the Egyptians; consistent with her representation as a cow, she produced the milk that became the celestial Milky Way.

During the millennia in which she was adored, she took on many roles and appellations, often conflated with goddesses like Isis and Nut, but fundamentally, Hathor was the generative principle of creation. In the words of Sir E. A. Wallis Budge:

> The texts prove that the worship of Hathor was also universal, and that her shrines were even more numerous than those of Horus. She was, in fact, the great mother of the world, and the old, cosmic Hathor was the personification of the great power of nature which was perpetually conceiving, and creating, and bringing forth, and rearing, and maintaining all things, both great and small. She was the "mother of her father, and the daughter of her son," and heaven, earth, and the Underworld were under her rule, and she was the mother of every god and every goddess. (Budge 2013, vol. 1)

Horus of Edfu

Edfu, formerly known as Behedet, is a word that comes from Coptic and means "city of retribution." Edfu was the principal cult center of Horus, known to the Greeks as Apollo, which is why they called the city Apollonopolis Magna.

The most important Ptolemaic temple dedicated to Horus, called Mesen, which means "the place of the harpoon," was built in Edfu. Today, this is one of the best-preserved temples in all of Egypt.

According to myth, Edfu was the site of the mythical battle in which Horus defeated Seth. Horus ascended into the sky in the form of a winged disk, representing the force of the sun at noon, and from the zenith he spotted the followers of Seth and descended upon them with such force that none of them survived. Horus was also the protector of the solar boat. He used a harpoon to slay crocodiles and hippopotamuses on the prow. The winged disk became his symbol, and it was placed at the entrance of many temples for protection.

The Edfu temple was closely related to the Temple of Hathor at Dendera as she was the wife of Horus. Each temple housed a statue of its deity. The Egyptians believed that the deity's *ba* (the part of the soul capable of traveling between the underworld and the world of the living) inhabited the temple statue.

Every year during the harvest season, priests of the Dendera temple celebrated a festival called the "Beautiful Reunion." A procession of boats carried the statue of the goddess Hathor up the Nile. Just before the full moon, the procession reached Edfu, where the statue of Horus awaited the arrival of the goddess. The pair of statues spent the night in the temple, where the deities consummated their reunion.

Nine months later, another festival took place at the Temple of Dendera, celebrating the birth of Horus and Hathor's son, Harsomtus (sometimes conflated with Ihy, other times his brother). He is usually depicted as a boy sitting on a lotus flower or playing the sistrum. He was born in the *mammisi* temple at the Dendera complex.

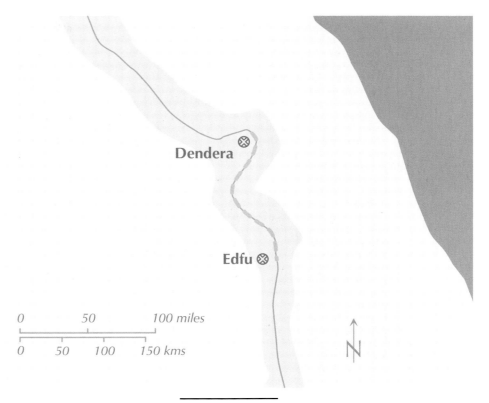

The Beautiful Reunion festival was celebrated every year with a procession up the Nile River from Dendera to Edfu.

Tanenet ⌒𓈖𓏏𓏏𓇳

Tanenet was the goddess of brewing. Her name comes from the word *tnmw*, which means "beer." Women in ancient Egypt were in charge of producing beer, which was consumed daily in large quantities as part of the daily diet. Egyptian beer was less alcoholic than modern beer but higher in caloric content. Beer was also used in religious ceremonies and had medicinal properties as an antibiotic. Wages were paid in beer, grain, and bread.

Tanenet was also a goddess of childbirth and protector of the womb during pregnancy.

She was depicted in human form, wearing the solar disk with the uraeus over her head.

Tanenet was one of the consorts of Montu, a powerful state-god protector of Thebes during the Eleventh Dynasty. Her main center of worship was at Hermonthis (modern-day Armant).

Iunit 𓇋𓃹𓈖𓏏𓉐

Iunit, along with Tanenet, was a fertility goddess and one of the consorts of the god Montu during the Eleventh Dynasty.

Her name Iunit means "she of Armant," a town south of Thebes (modern-day Luxor). Iunit was associated with the goddess Raet-Tawy, the female counterpart of the god Re.

A life-size granite statue of Iunit from the time of Amenhotep III was found in the Luxor temple in 1987.

At Dendera she is depicted wearing the Hathoric Horns.

West Panel I (days of the lunar month)

30th-Feast of heaven
Festival of Harendotes ("Horus, avenger of his father")

29th day-Training the companion
Celebration of the one who begets his father

28th day-Jubilee feast of heaven
Day of Khnum (fertility god, patron of Esna)

27th day-Answer
Festival of Dunanwi (a falcon god)

26th day-Emergence
Festival of Maaitef (a protector god of Osiris)

25th day-Light
Day of the emissary/ies

24th day-Darkness
Festival of Little Nay

23rd day-(Last) quarter
Festival of Great Nay

22nd day-Triangular junction
Festival of Nay

21st day-Provide
Festival of Anubis

20th day-Choice
Day of Wepwawet (Opener of the ways)

19th day-Hearing His Words
Day of Iunmutef ("Horus, pillar of his mother")

18th day-Moon, child

17th day-Knowledge
Festival of Horus on his papyrus stalk

16th day-Second refuge
Day during which obstacles are pushed back

Directly underneath the stairway in the scene of the Waxing of the Moon, there is an inscription with the names of the lunar days and the festival celebrated on each day of the month. The lunar month started with the new moon. The inscription reads from right to left.

15th day–Full Moon
Festival of Iremaway (protector of Osiris)

14th day–Wisdom
Festival of the majesty of Aries

13th day–See the light
Festival where we get closer to Re

12th day–Paths of light
Grinding day

11th day–Light
Festival of Hadjwer (Opener of the doors of the Duat)

10th day–Aspersion
Festival of Irrenefdjesef ("He who made his own name")

9th day–Fumigation
Festival of Irendjetef ("Whom his body made")

8th day–Eighth day
Festival of Manitef ("He who looks at his father")

7th day–First quarter
Festival of Qebehsenuef (Son of
Horus, protector of the intestines)

6th day–Sixth day
Festival of Duamutef (Son of
Horus, protector of the stomach)

5th day–Offering on the Altar
Festival of Hapi (Son of Horus, protector
of the lungs)

4th day–Going Forth of the Sem priest
Festival of Imsety (Son of Horus, protector of the liver)

3rd day–First refuge
Day of Osiris

2nd day–First day of the New Crescent
Festival of Harendotes ("Horus, avenger of his father")

1st day–New Moon
Festival of Thoth

Names of the 30 days
of the Lunar Month

The Full Moon

The last scene of the panel represents the full moon. Osiris is triumphant in his celestial boat accompanied by Isis and Nephthys, who are offering him the ankh, a symbol of life. A baboon sits at the prow of the boat. In front of him is Maat, the goddess of cosmic order, wearing a feather over her head. Horus Khenty-khety stands at the helm. Hovering above Osiris is Khepri, the sacred scarab representing the newborn sun (at sunrise). Khepri is standing on top of the *shen* on a scale made of ankhs and *was* scepters. At the end of the scale, light and darkness rest in balance.

Nekhbet and Wadjet, the tutelary deities (also present in the Central Panel), fly above, protecting Osiris.

The boat navigates over the sky, represented by the sky hieroglyph inscribed with thirty-six stars—the decans—supported by the four goddesses of the cardinal points. This alludes to the fact that the moon navigates all night over the sky when it is full, in contrast to the scene for the new moon where the boat navigates on the river above the ground, which is the blue sky representing its diurnal journey.

Three falcon-headed souls of Pe (Buto) and three jackal-headed souls of Nekhen (Hierakonpolis) surround the boat. All of them are striking their chests in a sign of jubilation at the full moon navigating from dusk to dawn.

Four pairs of frog- and snake-headed deities follow the boat. They are the Hermopolitan Ogdoad (from the ancient Greek ὀγδοάς "the Eightfold") and represent the elemental principles from which creation emerged. The four couples are Nu/Naunet, Heh/Hauhet, Kek/Kauket, and Nia/Niat. They represent the primordial waters, eternity, darkness, and void, respectively.

Closing the scene are the four-headed ram and the ram-headed bird, representing the winds of the south and west.

Contrary to Cauville and Priskin, Dr. Altmann-Wendling states that these kind of scenes does not match the typical full moon representations, but rather those that have the waning days of the lunar month as their subject (Mendel 2022, 288).

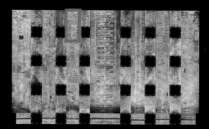

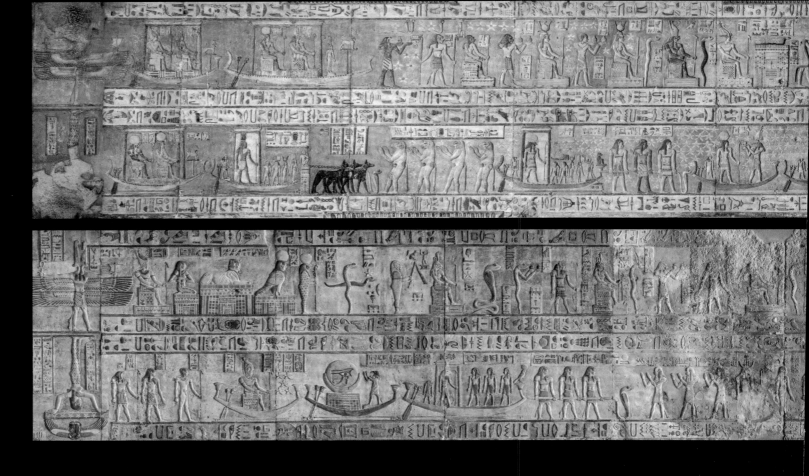

East Panel II and West Panel II

The two middle panels, East II and West II, are complementary.

The eastern panel (top) represents the day and the western one (bottom) the night. The sidebands with hieroglyphic texts are hymns dedicated to Sekhmet, Sothis, and Hathor. Each of the panels consists of an upper and a lower track.

The upper track of East Panel II contains the four winds, two boats carrying Isis, Osiris, Re, and Harsomtus, and the decanal stars 1 and 2 and 21 to 36.

The upper track of West Panel II contains decans 3 to 20.

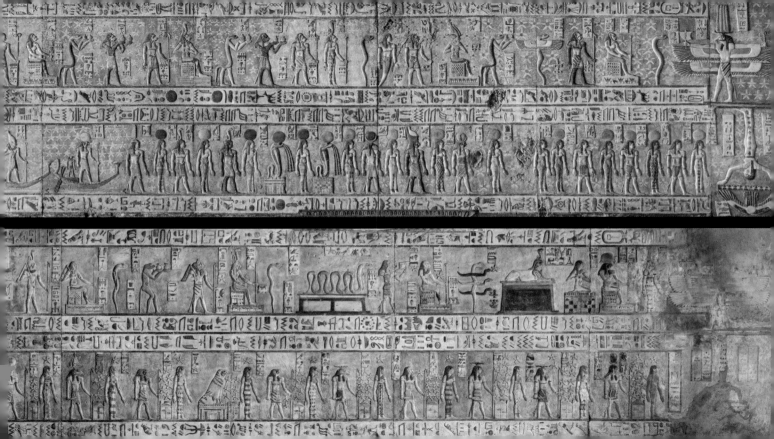

The Decans

The decans were groups of stars that divided the ecliptic into thirty-six parts. Each decan identified a week of 10 days, allowing three weeks for each month. Adding the 5 epagomenal days completed the full year of 365 days.

The first decan to appear on the eastern horizon at sunset marked the first hour of the night. As subsequent decans rose on the horizon, they marked the beginnings of the subsequent hours of the night. The first decan to rise at sunset changed every 10 days.

Among the writings describing the journey of Re through the Duat during the night, perhaps the most notable is the "Book of the Gates." It describes the solar boat passing through twelve gates during the night, to be reborn at dawn. A demon and his assistants guarded each gate.

Re was required to recite a spell at each gate and speak the name of the demon and his companions in order to pass. The brightest star in each decan represented the demon, and the pattern formed by the companion stars served to identify the specific decan. Memorizing the spells aided the priests in identifying the decans throughout the night.

During the Late Period, the use of decans to measure the night hours declined, giving way to the use of water clocks.

The decans helped to reckon the night hours and were also used to count the passing of weeks, months, and years. Some texts indicate their use to mark the times when meteorological phenomena such as seasonal winds, the flooding of the Nile, and the arrival of the scarce rains occurred.

During the Greco-Roman period, decanal amulets were used for healing and protection. These amulets were created using metals, minerals, or woods that were associated with each decan. The association between the decan and the material was based on the perceived qualities of the material, which were believed to reflect the qualities of the decan and its associated stars.

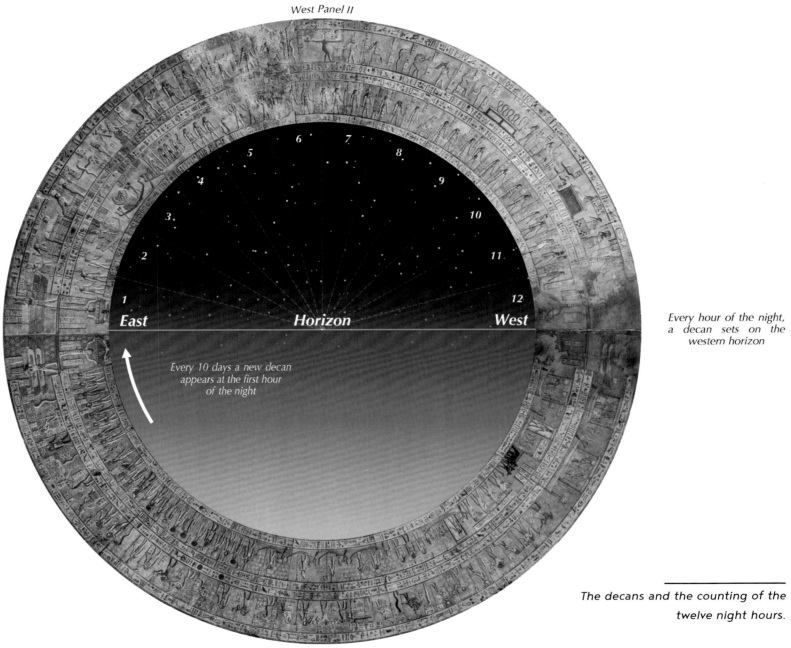

West Panel II

Every hour of the night,
a new decan appears on
the eastern horizon

Every hour of the night,
a decan sets on the
western horizon

Every 10 days a new decan
appears at the first hour
of the night

East   Horizon   West

The decans and the counting of the
twelve night hours.

East Panel II

East Panel II (upper track)

| **Good Wind of the East** | **Boat of Isis and Osiris**
The god Tutu, a human-headed standing lion, protects the boat at the prow. Seated inside the boat is Isis the great, the mother of the god. Behind her is Osiris, greater than the gods. | **Boat of Harsomtus**
Tutu protects the boat at the front. Behind him is Maat, the goddess of truth. Seated inside the boat is Harsomtus, son of Horus and Hathor. Behind him is Harsomtus again, master of the place of the lotus petal. | **Decan 2**
Setu
Material:
N/A | **Decan 1a**
Onuris
Material:
Granite | **Decan 1**
Sothis
Material:
N/A |

The left-hand side of the upper track of East Panel II starts with the Wind of the East, followed by two boats and the first three decans. If the name of the material associated with the decan is present in the track, it is mentioned below the decan's name. Sometimes more than one deity is used to represent a decan, in such cases, the corresponding decans are sublabeled a, b, and c.

East Panel II (upper track, the epagomenal days)

IX	VIII	VII	VI	V	IV	III	II	I
Senen	Nephthys	Ankhem-kheruy	Isis	Weshaty	Horus	Weshaty	Osiris	Weshaty
Material:		Material:		Material:		Material:		Material:
Wood, face in gold		Crystal, face in gold		Red stone, face in gold		Ebony, face in gold		Ebony, face in gold

The lunar year (12 lunar cycles) has 354 days. The upper track continues with 9 of the 11 additional days needed to complete the civil calendar of 365 days. Among these 9 days, 4 of the 5 epagomenal days are present. The missing epagomenal day was the day of Seth, excluded because his evil presence was deliberately exorcized from the temple. See the chapter "Nut and Geb" (above) for the myth of the epagomenal days as related by Plutarch.

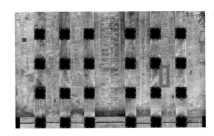

East Panel II (upper track, continuation)

Decan 36	Decan 35	Decan 34	Decan 33	Decan 32	Decan 31b	Decan 31a	Decan 31	Decan 30	Decan 29	Decan 28	Decan 27
Tepi-a Sopdet	*Waret*	*Reemhetep*	*Tjes-areq*	*Remen-hery*	*Aret*	*Semanebakhu*	*Khau*	*Saked*	*Khentu-kheriyew*	*Hertepnefer*	*Khentu-heriyew*
Material:	*Material:*	*Material:*	*Material:*	*Material:*	*Material:*	*Material:*	*Material:*	*Material:*	*Material:*	*Material:*	*Material:*
Ebony, face in gold	*Gold*	*Crystal, face in gold*	*Earthenware, face in gold*	*Crystal, face in gold*	*Granite, face in gold*	*Granite, face in gold*	*Carnelian, face in gold*	*Earthenware, face in gold*	*Jasper, face in gold*	*Earthenware, face in gold*	*Gold*

The right-hand side of the upper track of East Panel II shows the decans 36 to 21 and their associated materials and culminates with the Wind of the South.

Decan 26	Decan 25b	Decan 25a		Decan 25	Decan 24		Decan 23		Decan 22a		Decan 22		Decan 21			Southern Wind
Bawey	*Tepi-a Bawey*	*Wepwawet*		*Akhau*	*Tepi-a Akhwey*		*Kheri-kheped-seret*		*Wetetjimiut*		*Saseret*		*Seret*			*Southern Wind*
Material:	Material:	Material:		Material:	Material:		Material:		Material:		Material:		Material:			
Red and gold stone	**Gold**	**Carnelian, face in gold**		**Gold**	**Silver**		**Silver**		**Silver**		**Carnelian, face in gold**		**Dark flint, face in gold**			

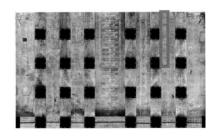

West Panel II (upper track)

Western Wind		*Atum*	*Pregnant woman*	*Atum sphinx*	*Atum-Re-Horakhty*	*Re-Horakhty*	*Decan 20*	*Decan 19a*
							Semed	*Kamermutef*
		Personifies the evening sun	*Sky that gives birth to Atum*	*Ka (life force) of Atum*	*Personifies the sun during its setting*	*Mummified falcon-headed god represents the sun on the western horizon at dusk*	*Material:* **Brass, face in gold**	*Material:* **Gold**

The track opens with the Western Wind. Atum is seated on his throne among other aspects of the evening sun, and to the right are the decans 20 to 12. (Illegible portions of names are marked with brackets.)

Decan 19	Decan 18	Decan 17	Decan 16a	Decan 16	Decan 15	Decan 14	Decan 13a	Decan 13	Decan 12
Tepi-a Semed	*Kenemu*	*Shesmu*	*Akhnekhakha*	*Heri-yeb wia*	*Sapty-khenwey*	*Tehemsu[khent]*	*Imsety[haty]*	*[Khentkheret]*	*Khentheret*
Material:	Material:	Material:	Material:	Material:	Material:	Material:	Material:	Material:	Material:
Gold	Carnelian, face in gold	Earthenware, face in gold	Earthenware, face in gold	Earthenware, face in gold	Flint	Earthenware, face in gold	Carnelian	Jasper, face in gold	Obsidian, face in gold

West Panel II (upper track, continuation)

Decan 11	Decan 10a	Decan 10	Decan 9	Decan 8a	Decan 8	Decan 7	Decan 6	Decan 5
Tepi-a Khentet	**Aapehty, Rehenpet**	**Sebekhes**	**Ipeset**	**Weshaty Bekaty**	**Setutrehenpet**	**Tjemat**	**Pehu-Djat**	**Het-Djat**
Material:	*Material:*	*Material:*	*Material:*	*Material:*	*Material:*	*Material:*	*Material:*	*Material:*
Magnetite	**Resin, face in gold**	**Earthenware, face in gold**	**Brass, face in gold**	**Turquoise**	**Bronze, face in gold**	**Gold**	**Black stone, face in gold**	**Earthenware, face in gold**

The decans continue, and the panel closes with the Northern Wind. The left-hand side of the upper track shows a medley of gods, and decans 11 to 3.

Decan 4a	**Decan 4**	**Decan 3**	**Sphinx**	**Nenet**	**Horus of Edfu**	**Maat**	**Northern Wind**
Khentu-heriyew	*Khery-kheped-Knumet*	*Knumet*					
Material:	Material:	Material:	Ka of the god Re	Sky goddess	The great	The great	
Turquoise,	**Earthenware,**	**Amethyst**	on a sarcophagus	who gave	god master	daughter of Re	
face in gold	**face in gold**			birth to Re	of heaven		

East Panel II (lower track)

Kyth	**Day journey boat of Re**	**Boat of Khepri**	**Souls of the East**	**4 Baboons worshiping Khepri**
Eastern pillar of the sky.	At the front, on the bow, is Tutu. Seated inside the boat are Hathor (lady of Dendera, the eye of Re, mistress of the sky) and Horus of Edfu, the great god master of the sky.	Khepri stands on the boat. A falcon-headed god at the helm steers the boat. Hu and Sia face Khepri. Hu, the god of taste, is the creative utterance of Atum. Sia is the deification of perception. The goddesses Hathor (or perhaps Isis) and Maat stand at the prow. In front of the boat, a child sucking his thumb sits on a pedestal.	Four jackals pull the boat out of the darkness of the night on the eastern horizon. In front of them, a cobra in a standing posture protects the boat.	Baboons were known for barking at dawn. They were usually depicted in early morning scenes barking, welcoming the sun.

This track represents the day. On the left is the eastern pillar of the sky. On the first boat is Re, the supreme diurnal being. Then comes the boat of Khepri, the sun at dawn. The boat of Re-Horakhty, the sun on the horizon, is next. The boat of the diurnal moon comes after, and then the other luminaries of the morning ride in their boats: Sirius, Orion, and Venus.

Boat of Re-Horakhty

Re-Horakhty ("Re who is
Horus of the Horizons")
stands on the boat as a falcon-
headed god with the solar disk
and the uraeus over his head.
Hu and Sia face the god.
Hathor and Maat stand
behind a falcon-headed god
who is spearing Apophis. A
baboon sits at the boat's prow.

The Tireless Ones

Three men pull the boat
into the southern sky. A
cobra in a standing
posture protects the boat.

Boat of the Moon

The god Thoth offers the
wedjat eye to the moon.

Boat of Sothis (Sirius)

Boat of Orion

Boat of the Morning God (Venus)

East Panel II (lower track, continuation)

1st hour	2nd hour	3rd hour	4th hour	5th hour	6th hour	7th hour
Hour name:	Hour name:	Hour name:	Hour name:	Hour name:	Hour name:	Hour name:
The one that shines	**The one that escorts**	**The one that protects her master**	**The one that is hidden**	**The one that burns**	**The one that is vertical**	**The one that chastises**
Protector:	Protector:	Protector:	Protector:	Protector:	Protector:	Protector:
Shu	**Hek**	**Sia**	**The flame**	**The uraeus**	**Thoth**	**Horus in joy**

The track continues with the twelve hours of the day, from dawn to dusk. Inverted, the goddess of the southern pillar of the sky closes the scene.

8th hour	9th hour	10th hour	11th hour	12th hour	Ahayt
Hour name:	*Hour name:*	*Hour name:*	*Hour name:*	*Hour name:*	*Southern pillar of the sky*
The one that exists	**The one whose image is splendid**	**The one whose form is illuminated**	**The one whose manifestation is healthy**	**The one whose splendor is hidden**	
Protector:	*Protector:*	*Protector:*	*Protector:*	*Protector:*	
Khonsu	**Isis**	**The great magician**	**The one who hauls the rope that holds the boat**	**The one that appears in the twilight**	

West Panel II (lower track)

Fayt	*Snake*	*The educated one*	*The god who is*	*Boat of Osiris*	*Boat of the full moon*

Fayt

*Western pillar
of the sky*

*Snake
of the nome*

*The educated one
who is in the water*

*The god who is
in heaven*

Boat of Osiris

*Osiris, who reunited with
the left eye, renews the moon's
cycle. It illuminates heaven
and earth in his perfection.
The five stars at the front are
the epagomenal days.*

Boat of the full moon

*The full moon containing the united
wedjat eye is being worshiped by Thoth.*

This track represents the night. On the left is the western pillar of the sky, inverted. Three stars and three boats open the track. Osiris and the moon, the regents of the night, travel in their boats. Atum, the evening sun, travels in his boat descending into the Duat.

Boat of Atum

Atum, the personification of
the evening sun.

Three men pulling the boat

A caption above the three men
mentions that "they are the stars who
accompany the sun in the northern sky."

Worshiping souls

Souls of the west who
welcome the solar barque.

West Panel II (lower track, continuation)

1st hour	2nd hour	3rd hour	4th hour	5th hour	6th hour	7th hour
Hour name:	*Hour name:*	*Hour name:*	*Hour name:*	*Hour name:*	*Hour name:*	*Hour name:*
Mistress of the twinkling stars	**The one who brings up her master**	**The one who keeps evil away**	**The one whose prestige is great**	**Mistress of life**	**The one whose image is splendid**	**The uraeus who fights for his master**
Protector:	*Protector:*	*Protector:*	*Protector:*	*Protector:*	*Protector:*	*Protector:*
Shiny bull	**Bull of the two lands**	**The one who shares the offerings**	**The one with the right face**	**Horus on his branch**	**Sokar**	**Morning Horus**

The right-hand side of the lower track contains the hours of the night and their protectors. The companion of the twelfth hour of the night is Khepri, last before dawn. The track closes with the northern pillar of the sky.

8th hour	9th hour	10th hour	11th hour	12th hour	Twait
Hour name:	*Hour name:*	*Hour name:*	*Hour name:*	*Hour name:*	Northern pillar of the sky
The one whose flame hurts	**Mistress of fear**	**The one who protects her master**	**The one who repels demons**	**The one who sees the perfection of her master**	
Protector:	*Protector:*	*Protector:*	*Protector:*	*Protector:*	
Aries	**Iunmutef**	**Master of the gods**	**The one who opens in his hill**	**Khepri**	

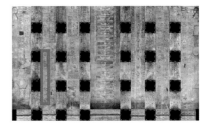

East Panel III and West Panel III

On the easternmost panel, the goddess Nut swallows the winged solar disk, which is reborn from her navel at dawn and rises over the Temple of Hathor at Dendera. The sun's rays touch the head of the goddess Hathor on top of a simplified image of the temple. This scene portrays the first day of the Egyptian new year, on which a statue of Hathor, retrieved from a crypt in the temple and placed on its roof, was rejuvenated by the first rays of the new year's sun.

The upper track of the panel contains six signs of the zodiac: Cancer (between Nut's legs), Gemini, Taurus, Aries, Pisces, and Aquarius. Since Nut's eyes are open on the panel, it means that these signs are "day" signs.

This track also includes deities representing the twelve hours of the night, the five planets known by the Egyptians, and other ancient Egyptian constellations.

East Panel III

The lower track of the panel displays figures standing or sitting in boats. These are the decans, thirty-six groups of stars near the ecliptic whose rise or transit could be used to determine the hour during the night. Astronomers also used them as place-markers in the sky to divide the ecliptic into equal portions.

The goddess Nut swallows a winged solar disk on the westernmost panel, which disk is reborn as a winged scarab.

The upper track of the panel contains the remaining six signs of the zodiac: Capricorn, Sagittarius, Scorpius, Libra, Virgo, and Leo. Since Nut's eyes are closed on the panel, these signs are "night" signs.

The upper track also portrays the twelve hours of the night, the five planets presented as birds, and additional ancient Egyptian constellations.

The lower track of the panel contains boats with deities representing the decans from 1 to 17 and 36.

The Annual Cycle

The outermost ceiling panels show the annual solar cycle. The mouth of the goddess Nut represents the western horizon where the sun sets to give way to the night. Her vagina represents the eastern horizon where the rising sun is born every morning. Nut's body is the celestial dome, the Nile in the sky, upon which the solar boat travels at night.

Just as the sun's diurnal journey is divided into morning and evening, the "annual day" also contains morning and evening phases. The "annual morning" begins on the winter solstice, the shortest day of the year, when the sun is at its lowest declination of the year. In the same way that the sun rises in the sky during the morning until it reaches its maximum altitude at noon, the sun ratchets higher in the sky during each day of the six "morning months" until it reaches its maximum elevation and power at the summer solstice. At the time of the Dendera temple, the summer solstice corresponded with the zodiac constellation of Cancer. The "morning" zodiacal constellations were Aquarius, Pisces, Aries, Taurus, Gemini, and Cancer.

The "annual afternoon" occurs over the next six months, during which the sun loses altitude daily until the next winter solstice, thus giving rise to the next cycle. The "evening" zodiac signs were Leo, Virgo, Libra, Scorpius, Sagittarius, and Capricorn.

The Egyptians celebrated the beginning of the year with the heliacal rising of Sirius, which marked the beginning of the flood just before the summer solstice. The turbulent red waters of the Nile came loaded with fertile sediments—the effusion of Osiris—and overflowed onto the banks of the river, fertilizing the land. When the waters receded, the black, moist soil was ripe for planting.

Nut swallows the solar disk at sunset.

Winter solstice in Capricorn. Shortest day of the year. Days become longer from here on.

As the water starts to recede, the moist fields are ready for planting

Autumn equinox in Libra. Day and night have the same length. Days become shorter than nights from here on.

Growing season

Maximum water level reached. As water recedes, it leaves fertile, arable land.

Inundation season

Evening / West Side of the Ceiling

Morning / East Side of the Ceiling

Water level of the Nile

Harvest season

Lowest water level reached. The land is dry, expectations for next flooding start to grow.

Nut gives birth to the solar disk at dawn in the form of the scarab Khepri.

Spring equinox in Aries. Day and night have the same length. Days become longer than nights from here on.

Summer solstice. Longest day of the year. Days become shorter from here on.

Because of the precession of the equinoxes, the summer solstice was in Cancer at the time of the temple's construction.

Heliacal rising of Sirius. Beginning of the ideal Egyptian Year. Beginning of the flooding of the Nile.

The outer panels depicting the seasons and the flooding of the Nile.

East Panel III (upper track)

The Temple of Hathor is rejuvenated by the sun's rays in the new year.	**Satet and Anuket**	**Sirius/Sopdet**	**Horus who is upon his papyrus stalk**	**Orion/Sah/Osiris**	**12th night hour** **She who protects her master**	**Gemini**

The easternmost panel starts with the constellation of Cancer, placed between the legs of the goddess Nut (see the section for Cancer/Khepri, p. 126). The upper track opens with the sun's rays shining upon the Temple of Hathor, followed by three boats. Then come interspersed the visible planets, additional ancient Egyptian constellations, the twelve hours of the night, a solar eclipse, and five constellations of the zodiac: Gemini, Taurus, Aries, Pisces, and Aquarius.

Gemini	11th night hour	10th night hour	Mercury		Taurus		9th night hour	8th night hour	Venus	Cassiopeia
	The one who repels demons	She who protects her master	The inert				Mistress of fear	The one whose flame hurts	The morning god	

East Panel III (upper track, continuation)

Aries	7th night hour	6th night hour	Jupiter	Solar eclipse	5th night hour	Pisces
	The uraeus who fights for his master	Mistress whose image is splendid	Horus who enlightens the earth		Mistress of life	

4th night hour	Mars	Aquarius	3rd night hour	2nd night hour		Saturn	1st night hour
The one whose prestige is great	Horus the Red		The one who keeps evil away	The one who brings up her master		Horus the bull	Mistress of the spheres

West Panel III (upper track)

1st night hour	Capricorn	Saturn	2nd night hour		The Big Dipper		3rd night hour	Jupiter	Sagittarius
Mistress of the spheres		(Shown as a falcon)	The one who brings up her master				The one who keeps evil away	(Shown as a falcon)	

The upper track of West Panel III displays interspersed several ancient Egyptian constellations, the five planets represented as birds, and six constellations of the zodiac: Capricorn, Sagittarius, Scorpius, Libra, Virgo, and Leo.

4th night
hour

5th night
hour

Mars

Scorpius

6th night
hour

7th night
hour

The one whose
prestige is great

Mistress of life

(Shown as
a falcon)

The one whose
image is splendid

The uraeus
who fights for
his master

West Panel III (upper track, continuation)

Venus	Libra	8th night hour	9th night hour	Mercury	Virgo	10th night hour	11th night hour
(Shown as a falcon)		The one whose flame hurts	Mistress of fear	The inert (Shown as a falcon)		The one who protects her master	The one who repels demons

This region of the track was damaged before the Napoleonic expedition to Egypt.

Leo

12th night hour

She who sees the perfection of her master

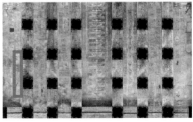

Nut, Death, and Rebirth

Just as the sun god descends at night to the underworld to be reborn the following day, the Egyptians, in their cyclical vision of the world, saw life and death as the day and night in which the deceased, when dying, crossed the horizon and descended into the underworld.

The starry night sky was the ocean where the mummified deceased sailed during death. For this reason, tombs and the interiors of the sarcophagi lids were decorated with star charts to guide the dead during the journey through the Duat.

The goddess Nut was the personification of the celestial dome, which the Egyptians perceived as a woman with an arched body, stretched out over her husband Geb, the earth.

Nut swallowed the sun at dusk, which sailed through her body during the night. Similarly, the stars traveled through the body of the goddess during the day. Nut gave birth to a new sun upon every sunrise.

The Milky Way, in predynastic times, looked like a woman stretched out on the celestial dome, with her arms and legs touching the earth.

In the early evening of the spring equinox, Nut's mouth appeared on the horizon where the sun descended. Six months later, during the autumnal equinox, the sun rises on the horizon at the point where the legs of the Milky Way fork.

The goddess Nut represented not only the sky but also regeneration. She swallowed an old and tired sun in the afternoon and gave birth to a new and rejuvenated sun every morning. In the same way, we descend tired to the underworld every night, where we travel through the world of dreams, from which we awake rested the following morning.

Since the sun rises in the east and sets in the west, the Egyptians associated the east with day, life, and wakefulness and the west with night, death, and sleep.

The Hathor temple at Dendera is oriented from north to south. The central corridor of the pronaos follows this axis and divides the room into two sides. The east side represents the day, and the west side represents the night. The outermost ceiling panels of both sides depict Nut arching her body with her arms and legs resting over the symbol of earth. Each version of the goddess wears a necklace with a winged beetle, Khepri, the symbol of self-generation and renewal. In addition, Nut in the east is wearing amulets with the eyes of Horus, further illustrating her connection to the hours of daylight. The wavy blue dresses of both versions of the goddess allude to the waters in the sky, like the Nile. However, in the east, Nut's eyes are open, representing the day, while in the west she sleeps with her eyes closed, symbolizing the night.

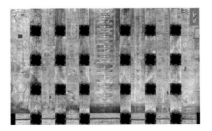

Cancer/Khepri

Cancer, "crab" in Latin, is the zodiac constellation between Gemini and Leo.

At the time of the creation of the Dendera temple, the zodiac would arrive at the summer solstice in Cancer. At the solstice, the sun stops moving north in the sky and begins to decline, or retreat, corresponding to the idea that crabs walk backward. In the two thousand years since the construction of the temple, because of the precession of the equinoxes, the constellations have shifted and the summer solstice now occurs under Gemini.

The Greeks believed that Cancer was placed in heaven by the goddess Hera for helping the hydra in her battle against Hercules.

At the northeastern corner of the ceiling of the Temple of Hathor, the scarab sits right beside the sun, having been born from the navel of the goddess Nut. The sun shines its first rays of dawn over the temple, represented as the inverted bovine face of the goddess Hathor.

Cancer has generally been associated with hard-shelled animals. The Babylonians represented it as a tortoise, and the Egyptians saw their sacred beetle, the scarabaeus, in it.

The scarab represents Khepri (meaning "the one coming into being"), the sun god at dawn, in charge of pushing the solar disk upward from the underworld into the morning sky.

Egyptians observed that beetles come out of the ground and roll dung balls from which new generations of beetles are born. They took this as a metaphor for the movement of the sun in the sky and its apparent spontaneous creation. Further embellishing the metaphor, the serrations on the heads of the beetles resembled the sun's rays.

The northwestern corner of the ceiling shows the god Khepri being born from the belly of the goddess Nut. The opposite panel on the northeastern corner shows Cancer being born from the belly of Nut. They represent the same scene—note the resemblance of the scarab and the crab.

The text on top of the winged scarab reads (translation from Cauville's French):

> *Horus of Edfu, the Great God Master of Heaven, falls into the western horizon, he takes possession of the Temple of the Menat Necklace [Temple of Hathor], his favorite place, he rests in the country-of-life, he joins his city. (It is) the primordial God shaped by Atum. The place of his powerful daughter on the floor of Geb, he spends the night there until dawn, it transforms into its Khepri form, it shows itself to the East, it illuminates the sky and the land of its beneficent Rays. (Cauville 2013a, 65)*

Gemini

The origin of the constellation of Gemini comes from the myth of Castor and Pollux. They were two half-twins, sons of the Aetolian princess Leda. Castor's father was the king of Sparta and Pollux's father was Zeus, who seduced Leda after assuming the form of a swan. The two brothers obtained immortality as the two brightest stars in the constellation of Gemini.

Gemini, which in Latin means "twins," lies between Taurus and Cancer, and above Orion. It is very prominent in the winter months of the northern hemisphere. It is one of the 48 constellations listed by the Alexandrian astronomer Ptolemy around 150 CE.

The ancient Egyptians identified the constellation as two goats, sometimes described as Horus the older and Horus the younger, and at other times simply called the "Two Stars."

In the ceiling of the pronaos of Dendera, Gemini is represented as the god Shu and his sister-consort Tefnut. (For more information on these two deities, see the chapter above, "Tefnut and Shu").

As we have seen, Shu represented dryness and preservation, while Tefnut represented moistness and change. Likewise, Gemini represented duality and complementarity, the union of opposites in harmony, illustrated in the scene from Dendera's temple by the two figures each reaching for the hand of the other.

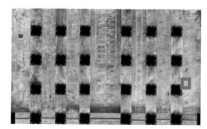

Taurus

The constellation of Taurus the Bull faces the sunrise and is located in the zodiac between Aries and Gemini.

In Babylonian and Egyptian records, the bull appears as the first constellation of the zodiac in 4000 BCE, when Taurus was the *princeps signorum coelestium* (chief of the heavenly signs)—the time when spring equinox occurred in that constellation. Due to the precession of the equinoxes, the constellations have shifted and the Spring Equinox is currently under Pisces.

In the Egyptian religion, the Apis bull was a primordial deity. His cult is known from the First Dynasty, and his center of worship was Memphis. Some accounts recognize him as the son of the goddess Isis, impregnated by the sun. Others claim that his mother was the goddess Hathor.

The priests of Memphis cared for one sacred bull at a time, the bull that represented Apis. When these bulls died, they were mummified and placed in giant sarcophagi in the underground necropolis at Saqqara. This cemetery was known as the Serapeum because it was one of the places of worship of the syncretic god Serapis, who was the union of the god Osiris and Apis.

> *The Apis, they say, is the animate image of Osiris, and he comes into being when a fructifying light thrusts forth from the moon and falls upon a cow in her breeding-season. Wherefore there are many things in the Apis that resemble features of the moon, his bright parts being darkened by the shadowy. Moreover, at the time of the new moon in the month of Phamenoth they celebrate a festival to which they give the name of "Osiris's coming to the Moon," and this marks the beginning of the spring. (Plutarch tr. 1927)*

Ptolemy I declared Serapis the patron of Alexandria, and his cult spread from Egypt into Greece.

Greek myths associate the constellation of Taurus with the insatiable lust of Zeus, their supreme god. On one occasion, Zeus fell in love with the princess of Tyre, Europa, whom he seduced after transforming himself into a bull. His constant infatuation for princesses led him to change Io, another of his lovers, into a heifer to hide her from his wife, Hera.

The bull is the quintessential spring symbol of youth and potency. "Bull of his mother Hathor" was a title for gods and pharaohs who were supposed to possess these qualities.

At the ceiling of the pronaos of Dendera, Taurus is depicted as a charging bull with a crescent moon on his back.

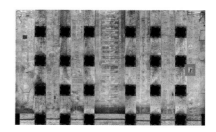

Aries

Aries means "ram" in Latin. Due to the equinoctial precession, after the Age of Taurus, around the second millennium BCE, the vernal equinox began to occur in the constellation Aries for the next two thousand years.

In Egypt, this time coincides with the prominence of the god Amun-Re, who displaced Montu as the patron of Thebes.

A long avenue flanked on both sides by two rows of ram-headed sphinxes connects the temples of Karnak and Luxor in the city of Thebes.

In Greek mythology, Aries is related to the Golden Fleece in the story of Jason and the Argonauts, recorded in the *Odyssey*. Numerous scholars propose that the voyage of the Argonauts symbolizes the path of the sun through the zodiac. According to this interpretation, Jason's quest to obtain the fleece represents the sun's journey through Aries.

After visiting the Temple of Zeus-Amun at the Oasis of Siwa, Alexander the Great proclaimed himself to be the son of the god. Subsequently, coins and statues depicted Alexander wearing the horns of a ram.

Given that the Egyptians worshiped the ram, they abhorred our own familiar concept of the "sacrificial lamb," as attested in Exodus:

> *And Moses said, "It is not right to do so, for we would be sacrificing the abomination of the Egyptians to the LORD our God. If we sacrifice the abomination of the Egyptians before their eyes, then will they not stone us?"* (Exodus 8:26, NKJV)

Pisces

Pisces is the Latin plural of the word for "fish." The Pisces constellation is between Aquarius and Aries in the zodiac. It is composed of a northern and a southern fish tied by their tails with a rope. The Age of Pisces began about two thousand years ago. We are now at the sunset of the Age of Pisces and are entering the Age of Aquarius.

According to Hyginus's *Poetic Astronomy,* Aphrodite and her son, Eros, were on the banks of the Euphrates River when Typhon (Seth) appeared. In order to escape, the pair jumped into the river, becoming fish tied with a rope so as not to lose each other. This ancient recounting is very similar to that of the *catasterism* (a Greek term meaning the transformation of a being into a star or constellation) of Capricorn.

On the ceiling of the pronaos of the Dendera temple, Pisces is depicted as two fish facing the same way with a rectangular pool in between.

Aquarius

Aquarius is a Latin word that means "water bearer." This constellation is located in the zodiac between Capricorn and Pisces.

According to the Greeks, Aquarius represented Ganymede, a young prince kidnapped by Zeus for his beauty and immortalized in heaven as the water carrier of the gods. Another Greek account suggests that Aquarius represented a spirit at the head of the Nile who regulated the flow of the waters by moving his feet.

On the ceiling of the pronaos of the Dendera temple, Aquarius is shown as the god Hapi pouring water from two vessels. Hapi represented the annual flooding of the Nile River, whose onset was called the "arrival of Hapi" by the Egyptians. This god was responsible for balancing the flood cycle of the river.

Hapi was depicted as a bearded, chubby man with a large breast—implying androgyny to some—symbols of the fertility, vitality, and abundance of the waters of the Nile. He wore a crown with lotuses or papyri, depending on whether he was being used to represent Upper or Lower Egypt.

Capricorn

Capricorn is a Latin word meaning "goat-horned." This constellation lies between Sagittarius and Pisces in the zodiac, and it is depicted as a goat-fish. The first images of a goat-fish are of Babylonian origin.

One Greek account explains the presence of this constellation in the zodiac as an homage from the god Zeus to Amalthea, the goat that suckled him.

Another myth recounts that the god Pan met Typhon (Seth) on the banks of the Nile and jumped into the river to escape from the monster. The submerged part of his body turned into the tail of a fish. Pan was the god of plenty. Therefore, the horn of Capricorn—the cornucopia—became a symbol of abundance.

Capricorn is shown as a goat-fish on the ceiling of the pronaos in the Temple of Dendera. Above it is the planet Saturn in the form of a bull-headed falcon.

When the temple was built, the sun was in Capricorn at the winter solstice. Due to the precession of the equinoxes, the winter solstice now occurs when the sun is in Sagittarius.

Capricorn is the last zodiac symbol in the upper track of West Panel III, and appears immediately before the goddess Nut swallows the winged solar disk at the last sunset of the year.

Sagittarius

Sagittarius, meaning "the archer" in Latin, is the constellation between Scorpius and Capricorn.

He is commonly depicted as a centaur archer. Detractors of this interpretation allege that centaurs did not use bows and arrows and that this figure is not qua-drupedal but bipedal. Hence, they identify Sagittarius with Krotos, a satyr son of the god Pan, and the inventor of archery.

This constellation is one of the most complex figures on the ceiling of the pro-naos of the temple. Sagittarius is depicted as a winged centaur with two tails, the upper one being the tail of a scorpion. He has two heads, one that is human and front-facing, and one that is leonine. He is crowned with the *atef* and points his arrow toward Scorpius. His front legs are inside a boat that represents the Corona Australis constellation.

Above him is a crowned falcon that signifies the planet Mars.

Scorpius

The Scorpius constellation is easily recognizable in the sky due to its size and the shape of its stars, which outline the curved tail of the scorpion.

Hyginus and Eratosthenes both recount the tale that describes how the scorpion ended up in heaven. Orion, the great hunter, decided to kill all the animals. To prevent this, Gaia, the goddess of the earth, sent a scorpion to sting Orion, who died from the poison. This explains why Scorpius and Orion are on opposite sides of the celestial dome—when Scorpius rises, Orion sets.

Scorpions were feared and respected by the Egyptians, as their venom could cause death by asphyxiation. Medical texts offered spells and potions to treat the stings.

Two pharaohs of the Protodynastic Period adopted the animal's name: Scorpion I and Scorpion II, each known as "King Scorpion."

The scorpion goddess was Serket, whose full name, *Serket hetyt,* means "she who causes the throat to breathe." She was the divine protector of poisonous bites and stings.

On the ceiling of the pronaos, the planet Mars appears above Scorpius in the form of a falcon crowned with the *hedjet,* a symbol of Upper Egypt. To the right is a green hippopotamus figure with a scorpion's tail, also wearing the *hedjet*. In both cases, the tail is composed by seven nodes, representing perhaps the seven brightest stars of the constellation's tail.

Curiously, the artists originally sculpted the scorpion with eight legs, which is the correct number for an arachnid. However, when applying the colors, for some unknown reason they decided to add an additional pair of legs.

Libra

The name for Libra the Scales comes from the Greek "*lítra*," which means "pound" and shares its origin with the word *liter*. All these words are related to measurement.

The sun was in the constellation of Libra at the autumnal equinox two thousand years ago. One should remember that the equinoxes are the two moments of the year in non-equatorial latitudes when day and night have the same length. Representing this moment of equivalence with the scales is appropriate, since the scales have been the symbol of fairness, balance, and justice from time immemorial. Libra is the only zodiac constellation whose symbol is not a creature but an object. Since the construction of the temple more two thousand years ago, the constellations have shifted due to the precession of the equinoxes and now the autumnal equinox occurs under Virgo.

The weighing of the heart is one of the most famous images in Egyptian mythology. Every being after death had to weigh their heart on a scale against the feather of Maat, a symbol of truth and justice, to prove that they were worthy of the afterlife. Osiris presided over the ceremony, Anubis weighed the heart, and Thoth recorded the outcome. The goddess Ammit watched the scene intently, ready to devour the heart if it did not balance with the feather. Ammit was an amalgamation of the most feared animals in ancient Egypt. She was part lion, part hippo, and had the head of a crocodile.

Libra is easily recognizable in the pronaos of the Temple of Dendera. The scales hover above a child poised inside the solar disk of the *akhet* ◠. The *akhet* was the hieroglyph for the horizon depicted as a rising sun above the mountains. Our current symbol for the constellation Libra ♎ comes from the *akhet*. The child sucking his finger inside the solar disk represents the new sun.

Virgo

The constellation of Virgo the Virgin is associated with the Greek myth of Persephone and her mother Demeter, goddess of the harvest and agriculture. Demeter was called Ceres by the Romans, whence the word *cereal*.

The young maiden Persephone (from the Greek Περσεφόνη "sheaf of corn," "grain," "seed") was abducted by Hades, god of the underworld. Demeter searched for her in vain and, in her sorrow, refused to grow vegetables, fruits, or cereals, leaving a desert wherever she went. Zeus intervened to order Persephone's release. From then on, she spent six months of the year in the underworld and six months with her mother. This myth provided an explanation for the changing of the seasons, with fall and winter being the times during which Persephone returned to the underworld.

The brightest star of the constellation is called Spica, Latin for "shaft," and represents the sheaf of wheat held by the virgin as portrayed in the pronaos of the Temple of Dendera.

Leo

The full power of the sun's heat coincided with the strength of the lion from around 4000 to 2000 BCE, as the summer solstice happened in Leo.

Its golden fur and mane, resembling solar rays, have reinforced its association with the sun since time immemorial.

According to the ancient Greeks, Zeus placed the lion among the stars to immortalize the bravery of Heracles, who killed the beast with his bare hands.

Leo is located between Cancer and Virgo in the zodiac and is one of the 48 constellations listed by Ptolemy during the second century CE.

Many Egyptians temples, including the Temple of Hathor at Dendera, use rain spouts shaped like the heads of lions, mirroring this description from Horapollo's *Hieroglyphica*:

> *To signify the rising of the Nile, which they call in the Egyptian language* NOUN *("Nun"), and which, when interpreted, signifies New, they sometimes portray a* LION, *and sometimes* THREE LARGE WATER POTS, *and at other times* HEAVEN AND EARTH GUSHING FORTH WITH WATER. *And they depict a* LION, *because when the sun is in Leo it augments the rising of the Nile, so that oftentimes while the sun remains in that sign of the zodiac, half of the new water [Noun, the entire inundation?] is supplied; and hence it is, that those who anciently presided over the sacred works, have made the spouts [?] and passages of the sacred fountains in the form of lions. (Cory 1840, XXI)*

In the ceiling of Dendera, Leo is depicted as a lion standing on a snake. In the night sky, directly underneath Leo is the constellation of Hydra, the Watersnake, slain by Hercules in one of his twelve quests.

Mercury

Mercury is the planet that is closest to the sun, which means that it can only be seen as an "evening star" on the western horizon just after sunset or as a "morning star" on the eastern horizon just before sunrise.

Known by the Egyptians as Sebegu, "the inert," Mercury was associated with Seth, perhaps because the planet was observed to accompany the setting sun to its "demise." Early texts show that Egyptians knew that the morning and evening stars were in fact the same celestial body.

On East Panel III, Mercury appears as a man holding the *was* scepter in one hand and an ankh in the other, crowned with a five-pointed star. Standing behind him is the tenth hour of the night.

On West Panel III (not shown), Mercury is between the ninth hour of the night and an unnamed bull-headed man holding a plow (probably another depiction of Virgo). There he is depicted as a baboon-headed bird. The baboon is one of the animals associated with the god Thoth, called Mercury by the Romans.

Venus

At first glance, we are confronted with a strange bicephalic creature, half-man, half-falcon, the man's head wearing the *deshret,* the red crown of Lower Egypt, and the falcon's head wearing the *hedjet,* the white crown of Upper Egypt.

Venus, one of the inner planets that orbits between the earth and the sun, can be seen only during the early morning or the late afternoon. The Greeks had different names for the morning and evening appearances of Venus: Phosphorus and Hesperus. Likewise, the Romans referred to them as Lucifer, the "light-bearer," and Vesper, meaning "evening," as in our word *vespertine.*

The Egyptians knew Venus as Bennu, "the morning star," a bird related to the god Re. It was said that Bennu died in flames and was born again every morning. Because of its death and resurrection, it became associated with Osiris. Bennu is probably the origin of the phoenix, the mythical Greek bird reborn from its own ashes.

On East Panel III, the Venus symbology on the ceiling of the Temple of Dendera is a beautiful and succinct example of the wisdom of the ancient Egyptians. It demonstrates that they recognized the morning and evening stars to be two different aspects of the same planet, united in harmony, like Upper and Lower Egypt. The bicephalic figure holds an ankh, a symbol of life, in one hand. In the other hand, he holds the *was* scepter, a symbol of power. To the right of Venus, a green baboon sits with a goat on its back, representing the constellation of Cassiopeia. To the left is the eighth hour of the night.

On West Panel III (not shown), Venus is shown to the left of Libra as a falcon wearing a *hedjet* crown, standing over a disk with a goddess inside wearing the same crown.

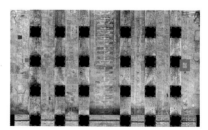

Mars

Mars is the Roman name of the god of war, known to the Greeks as Ares. Mars, the so-called red planet, is the first planet beyond Earth and is visible to the naked eye.

The Egyptians called Mars "Horus of the Horizon" or "Horus the Red" and described it as "the start which journeyeth backward in traveling."

From one night to the next, observers may report that a planet seems to have temporarily reversed its direction of travel during its journey along the ecliptic. This perceived backward travel, which is due to the difference between the orbital speed of the planet and Earth, is called "retrograde motion." Greeks called stellar bodies that exhibited this behavior "wanderers," which is the meaning of the word *planet*.

On East Panel III, Mars appears as a falcon-headed man holding the *was* scepter and an ankh, and crowned with a five-pointed star. He is between the fourth hour of the night and Aquarius.

On West Panel III (not shown), Mars appears as a falcon wearing a green *hedjet* crown and is above the constellation of Scorpius.

Jupiter

The planet Jupiter is the largest planet in the solar system and holds the Latin name of the head of the Roman pantheon of gods. He was known as Zeus by the Greeks.

Egyptians called Jupiter "Horus who limits the Two Lands" and gave him the epithet of "the southern star of the sky."

On East Panel III, Jupiter is portrayed as a falcon-headed man holding the *was* scepter and an ankh, and wearing the *atef* crown. He is between the sixth hour of the night and the solar eclipse.

On West Panel III (not shown), Jupiter appears over the constellation of Sagittarius as a bird wearing a feathered solar disk between two horns.

Saturn

Saturn is the Latin name for the furthest planet observable by the naked eye. Due to its distance from Earth, it also appears to be the slowest of the visible planets in its progression along the ecliptic. The Greeks knew Saturn as Cronos, the god of time. The Egyptians called it "Horus bull of Heavens," and gave him the epithet of "star of the east who traversed heaven."

On East Panel III, Saturn appears as a bull-headed man holding the *was* scepter and an ankh. He stands behind the first hour of the night. Behind him is an unnamed falcon-headed deity standing over a goose.

On West Panel III (not shown), Saturn is a bull-headed bird over the constellation of Capricorn.

The Big Dipper

Ursa Major, known colloquially as the Big Bear, is probably the earliest-named constellation. It is recognized by the brightest seven stars that fall on the back and tail of the bear. Human imagination has projected upon these stars a plethora of images. The Babylonians saw them as a wagon. The Romans saw seven plowing oxen. In Europe, they were seen either as a horse-drawn wagon or as a plow. The North American Sioux associated them with a skunk. In North Africa they were seen as a camel, in Siberia as a moose, and in the East Indies as either a shark or a canoe. The Chinese saw them as a scene wherein their god of literature, Weng-chang, granted an audience to his supplicants. Today we know them simply as the Big Dipper.

The Egyptians called these seven stars Meskhetyu and associated them with the leg of a bull or with an adze, similar to the one used in the "Opening of the Mouth" ceremony, performed to enable the deceased to eat and drink in the afterlife. The "Book of the Dead" (a set of funerary texts from the beginning of the New Kingdom) refers to these stars as the "thigh in the northern sky."

The stars of the zodiac disappear throughout the year and return; they mark the seasons. These stars rise and set and herald the birth of the sun.

In contrast, the circumpolar stars are visible every night of the year, and so the Egyptians called them "the Imperishables." Each star of Meskhetyu is one of these circumpolar stars.

Since these stars are only present in the darkness of night, they were associated with the god Seth. The myth of Horus defeating Seth represents the light of the rising sun destroying the circumpolar stars.

The Jumilhac papyrus (a long manuscript describing early Egyptian myths, currently housed at the Louvre) says that Horus severed the leg of Seth and threw it into the sky so that it could not harm Osiris, while a hippopotamus accompanied the leg so that it could not escape from the northern sky.

This is described by Norman Lockyer, as read from an inscription on a king's grave at Thebes:

> *The constellation of the Thigh appears at the late rising. When this constellation is in the middle of the heavens, having come to the south, where Orion lies [Orion typifying the southern part of the skies], the other stars are wending their way to the western horizon. Regarding the Thigh; it is the Thigh of Seth, so long as it is seen in the northern heavens there is a band [of stars?] to the two [sword handles?] in the shape of a great bronze chain. It is the place of Isis in the shape of a Hippopotamus to guard. (Lockyer 2006)*

The scene at Dendera shows Meskhetyu as the foreleg and the head of the bull surrounded by the seven stars. The hippopotamus chaining the foreleg is Taweret. She can be recognized holding her symbol, the *sa* ⚲. Spearing the leg is the falcon-headed god Anu.

The Solar Eclipse

In 52 CE, while the ceiling of the pronaos was being decorated, a conjunction between the earth, the moon, and the sun took place, creating a total solar eclipse in Alexandria. This troubling event, visible from Dendera, was recorded for posterity on the ceiling of the temple.

Eclipses were represented by a pig swallowing the solar disk. In Egyptian mythology, the pig symbolized evil and was associated with Seth, likely because of its filthy habits and diet. In a conversation with Egyptologist Manon Y. Schutz, she pointed out that hippopotamuses were seen as water pigs, which might be another reason why pigs were related to Seth.

The eclipse is shown as a large solar disk with a green man inside, holding a pig by its hind legs. He holds an ankh in the other hand. The scene is framed by Pisces and Aries, the region of the zodiac where the eclipse occurred.

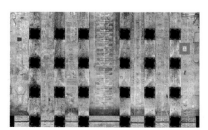

Sirius/Sothis

The star Sirius—the Dog Star—is about 8.6 light-years away from Earth, and it is about twenty-five times brighter than the sun. Its luminosity and relative closeness to our planet make Sirius the brightest star in the sky.

Sirius rests on the head of the constellation Canis Major (the big dog).

The heliacal rising of Sirius occurs annually when it first becomes visible on the horizon at dawn after a period of invisibility of about seventy days.

Given the influence of the inundation of the Nile on Egyptian life, perhaps the astronomical discovery with the most impact on the Egyptians was to notice that the heliacal rising of Sirius coincided with the beginning of the flooding. This observation had a profound effect on their myths, religion, rituals, and time measurement.

Sirius was known by the Greeks as Sothis, from the Egyptian name Sopdet, meaning "triangle."

Sothis was conflated with the goddess Isis, becoming Isis-Sothis. One of her epithets was "bringer of the New Year and the Nile Flood," an allusion to Sirius/Sothis as a sign of the imminent floods. The festival celebrating the heliacal rising of Sirius was called Wepet-Renpet, "Opening of the Year."

At Dendera, Sothis is depicted as a resting cow on a boat with a star between her horns. No doubt this was an allusion to the star Sirius.

Above the boat, the text reads:

> *Sothis the great, mistress of the stars, Isis mistress of the sky, shining at the beginning of the year to usher in a happy year, which flows peacefully behind her brother, Orion, while her son Horus is the King of Upper and Lower Egypt, forever. (Cauville 2013a)*

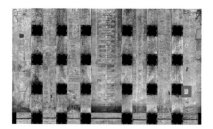

Orion/Sah

The mighty Orion is one of the most conspicuous constellations in the starry night. The Greeks saw in this constellation a giant hunter. Its seven brightest stars form its signature hourglass shape. The three central stars form a line known as "Orion's Belt."

Ancient Egyptians identified it with the god Sah, husband of the goddess Sothis and father of the falcon god Sopdu.

The triad of Sah-Sothis-Sopdu became assimilated over time by Osiris-Isis-Horus. Orion rises immediately before Sirius, heralding its coming. This is a significant event since the heliacal rising of Sirius marks the beginning of the inundation of the Nile.

At Dendera, Orion is depicted as Osiris standing on his boat, looking back at his beloved Sothis-Isis in the form of a resting cow. Between them is the star Canopus, their celestial heir, shown as a falcon standing on a papyrus stem wearing the double crown. In front of Orion's boat, facing it, is the twelfth hour of the night—the hour before dawn, signaling the heliacal rising.

Satet and Anuket

The island of Elephantine, located on the Nile downstream of the First Cataract, marked the border between Nubia and Egypt and was the center of trade routes where exotic products from the southern regions of Africa arrived in Egypt. Products like elephant ivory were traded here; hence the name Elephantine.

According to Egyptian mythology, the Nile originated in caves under the island and was protected by the primordial god Khnum, who, together with the goddesses Anuket and Satet, made up the Elephantine triad.

Anuket, originally a Nubian deity, was the goddess of the Aswan Cataracts. She wears a crown made of feathers. At Dendera, she is pouring water from two jars, similar to the image of the constellation Aquarius. Anuket was a fertility deity, and the animal associated with her was the gazelle.

The goddess Satet, known to the Greeks as Satis, personified the annual flooding of the Nile. Satet wears the crown from Upper Egypt with antelope horns, the antelope being the animal associated with the goddess.

With their quick movements and leaps, the gazelle and the antelope evoke the rapids and dangerous whirlpools formed in this region of the river.

The boat of Anuket and Satet, located on the ceiling between Sothis and Cancer, alludes to the flooding of the Nile. The heliacal rising of Sothis, a celestial event, marks and influences the flood, and thus, the beginning of the cycle of fertility and life on earth, just before the summer solstice, represented by the crab.

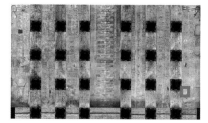

East Panel III (lower track)

| Sun at dawn | Snake in the lotus Harsomtus | Isis the great | Hathor the great | Ihy the great, son of Hathor | Decan 35 Waret | Decan 34 Remen-khery | Decan 33 Tjes-areq |

| Decan 27 Khentu-kheriyew | Decan 26 Khentu-heriyew | Decan 25 Tepi-a Bawey | Decan 24 Bawey | Decan 23 Tepi-a Bawey |

The lower track of East Panel III starts with the sun at dawn being born out of Nut, followed by two boats representing constellations. The first boat holds a snake rising from a lotus flower. It represents Harsomtus, the child of Hathor and Horus of Edfu. Lotus flowers open in the morning with the sun's first rays, hence their association with the dawn.

Decan 32
Remen-hery

Decan 31
Aret

Decan 30
Khau

Decan 29
Saked

Decan 28
Kedkhau

Decan 22
Akhwey

Decan 21
Tepi-a Akhwey

Decan 20
Saseret

Decan 19
Semed

Decan 18
Pa-sebu-wity

Sun at
sunset

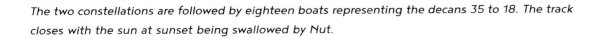

The two constellations are followed by eighteen boats representing the decans 35 to 18. The track
closes with the sun at sunset being swallowed by Nut.

West Panel III (lower track)

Sun at sunset	Decan 17	Decan 16	Decan 15	Decan 14	Decan 13
	Tepi-a Semed	*Kenemu*	*Sa-shesmu*	*Shesmu*	*Sept-henu*

Decan 7	Decan 6	Decan 5	Decan 4	Decan 3
Weshaty	*Tem*	*Pehu-Djat*	*Djat*	*Het-Djat*

The lower track of West Panel III (read from right to left) shows the sun at dawn represented by a winged scarab, followed by boats representing the decans 36 and 1 to 17. The track closes with the sun at sunset being swallowed by the goddess Nut. Decan 13 was not cleaned to show the black soot that accumulated over the years (see appendix B).

Decan 12
Heri-yeb wia

Decan 11
Tepi-a Khentet

Decan 10
Sebekhes

Decan 9
Ipeset

Decan 8
Baked

Decan 2
N/A

This section of the track was damaged
from before the Napoleonic expedition to Egypt.

Decan 1
Ihy

Decan 36
Pehwey-hery

Sun at dawn as
a winged scarab

Epilogue

In June 2022 I decided to return to the temple. It isn't easy to describe the feeling of being under its canopy again. Perhaps the closest emotion I have had was the one I once felt in a zoo with my daughters, where a few steps away from us was a silent giraffe. The simple existence of this animal is a miracle. It is an impossible and fragile creature, yet at the same time, it is eternal and powerful. It is an embodied paradox that should not exist, yet it does. The Dendera temple exudes a similar feeling. The vibrant colors and delicate figures in perfect condition are antithetical to their age. Like the giraffe, the temple creates a paradoxical state of something that should not exist, yet does indeed exist.

No matter how many photos, videos, or descriptions of the temple are made, the feeling of being there in person is inexpressible. Looking up and observing its ceiling, the enormity of its columns, and the magnificence of its colorful images and hieroglyphs evokes the ancient presence of the divine cow, Hathor. Despite the incessant flow of time, desert sandstorms, and waves of monotheistic intolerance and its chisels, her magnificence remains unerased. Her womb is the theater in which the drama of existence takes place and which she silently regenerates and feeds.

After spending some time in Egypt and having lived with the Nile, its vegetation, its animals, and its people, the apparently incomprehensible images on the walls of its tombs, monuments, and temples began to make sense. The civilization that developed in ancient Egypt is a fruit of the river, the sun, and the desert, just like the dates that grow on the palm trees. Its elaborate symbology is an expression of the human intellect that has managed to distill the divine essence of the oasis and its creatures and to transmute it into sacred writing and animal gods.

Today we live in a desert populated by cold and inert objects that we hoard and dispose. Instead, the ancient Egyptians inhabited a universe not made of things but of meaning. Even the smallest animals and mundane utensils of daily use were imbued with the essence of their gods. Every action, every object, and every word had a sacred aspect. Their world was not the dwelling place of the gods; their world was the sum of the divine properties of the gods.

The sun, which makes life possible, also causes the desert's aridity and death. The Nile, which brought fertility to the arid lands of the desert, also, in excess, brought destruction and pestilence. The Egyptians saw prosperity in the balance of opposites. Their lives depended on this order they called Maat, the image of which was the balance weighing the heart against the feather. For the Egyptians, everything had a meaning and a place in the universal order. Even Seth, who represented the death of the desert, was the one who protected their civilization from foreign invasions.

We conceive of time as a linear succession of impersonal and cold instants. Instead, Egyptian time had texture: it was a river of emotions and qualities repeating daily, monthly, and annually. Thus, the hours of the day were not just a numerical partition of the solar movement in the sky but were the flow of the qualities of their god Re during the day: the warm young child at dawn, the scorching sun at noon, and the weak evening sun before it died and plunged into the darkness of night. In the same way, the month, measure of the lunar cycle, was the dismemberment and reconstitution of Osiris, the perfect symbol of the drama of life and death. The year was the pulsation of the Nile expanding over its banks, fertilizing and bringing life with its flood, and the contraction and aridity during drought.

Ancient Egyptian ideas and deities were so powerful that even in ruin and after thousands of years, they still capture the imagination of millions of travelers annually and contribute integrally to modern Egypt's economy and identity.

We can only grasp a small part of the symbolic and emotional richness of the world that the ancient Egyptians inhabited. Still, the monuments they left behind remind us that there are rich, meaningful, and alternative ways of understanding the world and who we are.

Egyptian Iconography

Our emphasis on reason and literal interpretation is powerless when confronted with the unusual and terrifying Egyptian gods. Through Western eyes, they often seem incomprehensible and can only be characterized as the products of the imagination of superstitious and primitive beings. However, a society forced to inhabit a brutal environment like the Egyptian desert, capable of creating the most enduring civilization humanity has ever known, cannot be founded on superstition and mindless fantasy.

Thanks to the genius of Champollion and the discovery of the Rosetta Stone, we can decipher its mysterious writing. However, it is one thing to be able to read it and another to understand it. When confronted by exotic texts that we cannot comprehend, the usual reaction is one of dismissal, resorting to labeling the authors as superstitious and primitive. One may wonder exactly who is being superstitious and primitive.

Most Egyptian knowledge was secret and learned orally by initiates of different cults. Many of the connotations of Egyptian iconography will perhaps forever elude us.

Ancient Egyptians created an incredibly elaborate pictorial language. Their otherworldly and unusual-looking deities are not meant to be taken literally.

Plutarch notes in his *Moralia,* volume 5:

> *Nothing that is irrational or fabulous or prompted by superstition, as some believe, has ever been given a place in their [the Egyptians] rites, but in them are some things that have moral and practical values, and others that are not without their share in the refinements of history or natural science. (Plutarch tr. 1927)*

Like heraldry, Egyptian iconography is an abstract language of visual elements meant to be read and interpreted as qualities associated with the characters being represented.

Whether the figures are human, animal, or hybrid, their clothing, crowns, scepters, posture, number, and color are all carefully composed so as to create a deliberately rich qualitative unit.

For example, when animals are depicted, they represent characteristics possessed by those animals: the cow is nurturing, the lioness is fearless, and the falcon is agile and keen-sighted.

On the page opposite we see some examples of the ancient Egyptians' iconography of crowns. The seemingly overwhelming diversity is in fact built upon just a few fundamental components.

Among the most common components we see the *hedjet,* associated with the vulture and Upper Egypt, and the *deshret,* associated with the cobra-uraeus and Lower Egypt. In addition, we see the ostrich feather as a symbol of truth, the solar disk, and the horns of cows and rams. For example, the *atef* (usually worn by Osiris) is the *hedjet* with two ostrich feathers. The double crown, called the *pschent,* is shown in the center image. It is the union of the *hedjet* and the *deshret* and represents the unification of Upper and Lower Egypt.

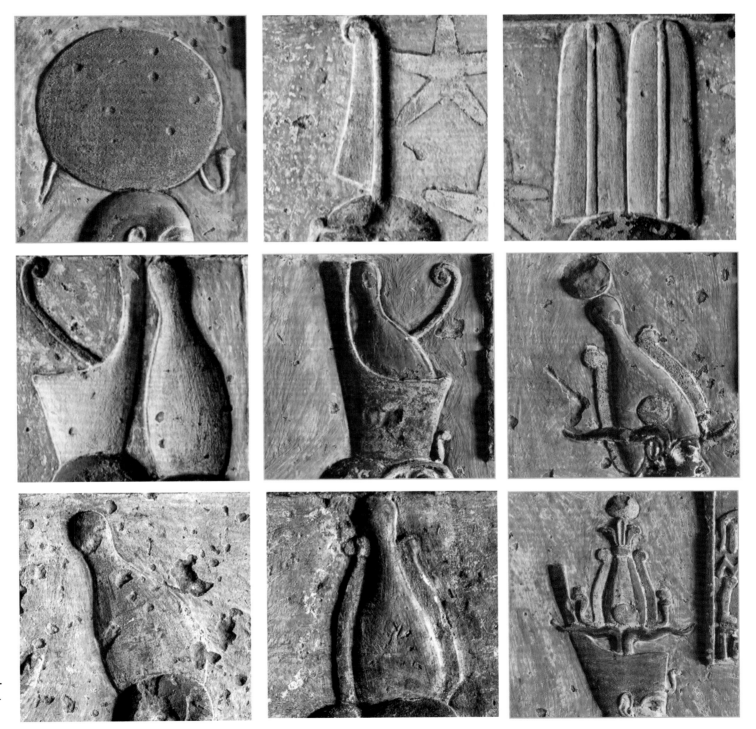

Crowns of ancient Egypt.

Back to Life

After the decline of the ancient Egyptian civilization, the Temple of Hathor at Dendera was abandoned. Bedouins began to inhabit its spaces and lit fires to shelter from the cold of the nighttime desert. When the French Napoleonic expedition found the temple half-covered in sand at the turn of the nineteenth century, its once-magnificent ceiling was mostly covered in layers of black soot.

Egypt's Supreme Council of Antiquities began the temple's restoration in 2005. This work was paused after six years and resumed again in 2017.

Today we can see that the temple's diligent conservators have managed to bring back to life the radiant and beautiful colors hidden beneath the centuries-old layers of soot from the fires of the Bedouins. The dominant color is blue, but the polychromy is varied, with shades of green, brown, red, black, white, and yellow all playing upon the sandstone surfaces.

13th decan, Sepetkhenu, on the lower track of West Panel III. It is the only part of the ceiling deliberately left untouched by the restorers.

APPENDIX C
The Taken Ceiling

The Circular Zodiac of the Temple of Hathor at Dendera is carved into two large stone slabs displaying all the constellations of the zodiac.

Dominique Vivant, Baron Denon, one of the savants of Napoleon's expedition to Egypt, first saw these magnificent stones in 1799 in a small chapel on the temple's roof.

Astronomers believed they could use the presented arrangement of the stars in the zodiac to date the ceiling. The Circular Zodiac caused great interest and controversy in Europe since its date could have potentially contradicted biblical dates at a time of anti-Catholic fervor in France.

Sébastien Louis Saulnier, an antiques dealer, commissioned Claude Lelorrain to remove the Circular Zodiac with saws, jacks, scissors, and gunpowder.

The removal was authorized by Muhammad Ali, an Ottoman military commander of Albanian origin, who was the governor of Egypt at the time and who had no particular interest in the ancient heritage of the country.

The zodiac was transported from Egypt in 1821. In 1822 Saulnier sold the zodiac to Louis XVIII for 150,000 francs, who installed the ceiling at the Royal Library in Paris. In 1922, the zodiac was moved to the Louvre, where it currently resides.

The hole left in the roof of the temple's chapel was later covered with a plaster replica of the Circular Zodiac.

The Temple of Dendera is one of the best-preserved examples of Ptolemaic architecture in all of Egypt. The absence of the Circular Zodiac is a reminder of the colonialism and plunder of antiquities to which Egypt has been subjected for millennia. The Egyptian government has asked for its return without success.

Illustration of the Circular Zodiac of Dendera.

Jollois and de Villiers from the Description de l'Égypte.

Plaster reproduction of the taken ceiling, replacing the original.

APPENDIX D
The *Description de l'Égypte*

One can only imagine what went through Napoleon Bonaparte's head when, in 1798, at age twenty-nine—and following in the footsteps of Alexander the Great—he landed in Alexandria accompanied by 35,000 soldiers. The biggest obstacle to his imperial ambitions was the British Empire. The objectives of the campaign in Egypt were primarily to block the British trade routes with India. Like the Romans eighteen centuries previously, capturing Egypt would have enabled the French to become the owners of the wealth of the Nile. This ownership would have become the breadbasket of the French Empire. Another important objective was to recover as much knowledge from ancient Egypt as possible, an unsurprising goal given the influence of the Age of Enlightenment.

For this purpose, the 151 civilians who accompanied Napoleon on his campaign established the Commission des Sciences et des Arts upon landing in Alexandria. Artists, mathematicians, astronomers, and architects, among others, were tasked with traveling around Egypt to study the ancient ruins and monuments. After several battles, Napoleon took Egypt. However, in August of 1798, in the Battle of the Nile, the British Navy destroyed the French fleet, leaving Napoleon and his soldiers trapped in Egypt. In March 1799, Napoleon quietly made his way back to France, leaving his soldiers and scholars behind. The campaign finally concluded with the French capitulation at Alexandria in 1801. The terms of surrender included the repatriation of the French back to their homeland in British ships.

Militarily, the campaign in Egypt was a disaster. Its only useful legacy to the French was the knowledge collected by Napoleon's scholars during their years in Egypt.

Their most famous discovery was the Rosetta Stone, which contributed to the revival of the study of Egyptian hieroglyphs, unlocking many of the secrets that until then were indecipherable.

Under Napoleon's orders, the compiled findings were published in a grandiose series of twenty-three volumes called the *Description de l'Égypte,* with 894 plates containing more than 3,000 illustrations.

Its publication in 1809, and the publication of diaries from some members of the Commission recounting their adventures, helped spark a European obsession with ancient Egypt.

DESCRIPTION
DE L'ÉGYPTE,

OU

RECUEIL

DES OBSERVATIONS ET DES RECHERCHES

QUI ONT ÉTÉ FAITES EN ÉGYPTE

PENDANT L'EXPÉDITION DE L'ARMÉE FRANÇAISE,

PUBLIÉ

PAR LES ORDRES DE SA MAJESTÉ L'EMPEREUR

NAPOLÉON LE GRAND.

———

ANTIQUITÉS, PLANCHES.

TOME PREMIER.

A PARIS,

DE L'IMPRIMERIE IMPÉRIALE.

M. DCCC. IX.

Title page of the first edition of the
Description de l'Égypte, *1809.*

APPENDIX E
French Savants' Depictions of the Ceiling

Dominique Vivant, Baron Denon, was an aristocrat and polymath, and one of the most influential members of Napoleon's Commission des Sciences et des Arts.

Denon was one of the first Frenchman to arrive at Dendera. On the temple's roof, he found the famous Circular Zodiac in one of its chapels, and immediately recognized its importance to the study of astronomy:

> *I had just discovered, in a small apartment, a celestial planisphere, when the last rays of day-light made me perceive that I was alone here, along with my kind and obliging friend General Beliard. . . . From the window of my apartment at Keneh, I saw the ruins of Tentyra, two leagues off, on the other side of the Nile; those ruins, the recollection of which inspired me with so much interest, mixed at the same time with regret, at not having had an opportunity to make a drawing of a zodiac, which clearly proved the deep knowledge of the ancient Egyptians in astronomy. (Denon 1803)*

He would have a chance to reproduce the ceilings in a later visit to Dendera. Denon managed to escape with Napoleon to France. In 1803, he published his memoirs of the trip, which took Europe by storm. Napoleon gave him the title of Baron and appointed him director of the Louvre.

Two other members of the Commission were instrumental in the creation of the *Description de l'Égypte*: Jean-Baptiste Prosper Jollois and Édouard de Villiers du Terrage.

Jollois and de Villiers had a chance to spend more time in Dendera than Denon

and created more detailed renditions of the ceilings. They were also responsible for the discovery of the tomb of Amenhotep III.

In his diary, de Villiers described the conditions in which they had to work at Dendera:

> *We wanted to have a faithful representation of it, allowing us to study exactly the astronomical knowledge of the ancient Egyptians. This work was long and painful; placed in a small chamber built on top of the great temple, the zodiac is found in almost complete darkness. We had to copy it, mostly with bad lights. As it is on the ceiling and very blackened by a kind of smoke, to clearly discern a sign we often had to look for long moments in a most uncomfortable position. We started by dividing it into eight equal sectors by threads stretched horizontally on the ceiling. Finally this long work was finished to our complete satisfaction. (Villiers 1899)*

Another passage from his diary is quite revealing regarding the attitude of the French savants in Egypt:

> *But what above all presents a very picturesque effect and a very striking contrast are the remains of modern houses which are as if suspended in the air on the terraces of the temple. An Arab village, composed of miserable earthen huts, dominates the most magnificent monument of Egyptian architecture and seems placed there to attest to the triumph of ignorance and barbarism over the centuries of light which have raised in Egypt the arts to the highest degree of splendor. (Villiers 1899)*

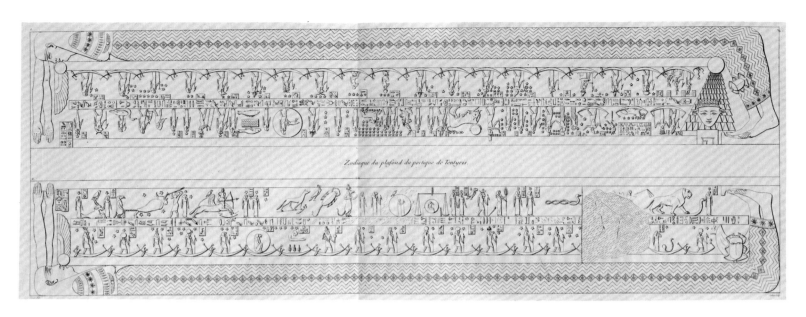

Renditions from the pronaos's ceiling of the temple of Dendera by Dominique Vivant Denon. He was challenged with time constraints, poor lighting conditions, and the fact that the ceiling was covered in centuries of soot. For these reasons, his renditions contain many inaccuracies. All figures in his East Panel III are facing in the wrong direction.

Notice in the upper left corner of the bottom track Denon mistakes the south wind, a four-headed winged ram, for a bicephalic pegasus.

The middle panel is an equivalent scene from the temple of Apollonopolis Magna (Edfu).

Denon missed the scene that goes between the last two scenes in the track of the moon.

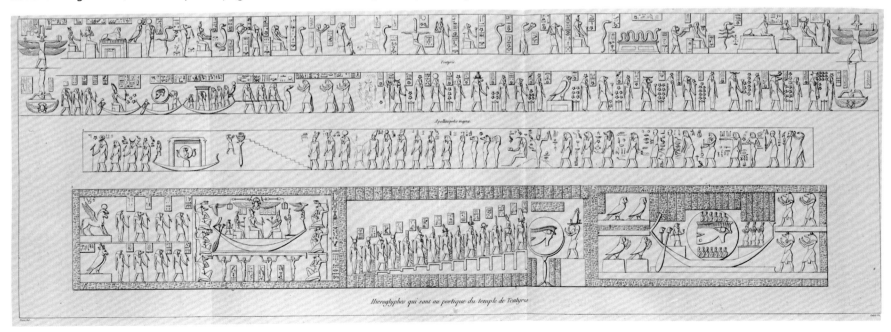

Illustrations of East Panel III and West Panel III of the
pronaos's ceiling of the temple of Dendera by Jollois
and de Villiers from Description de l'Égypte, vol. IV, plate 20.

Illustrations of East and West Panels I and II of the
pronaos's ceiling of the temple of Dendera by Jollois and
de Villiers from Description de l'Égypte, vol IV, plate 19.

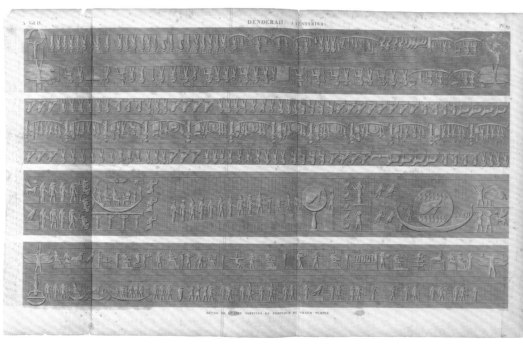

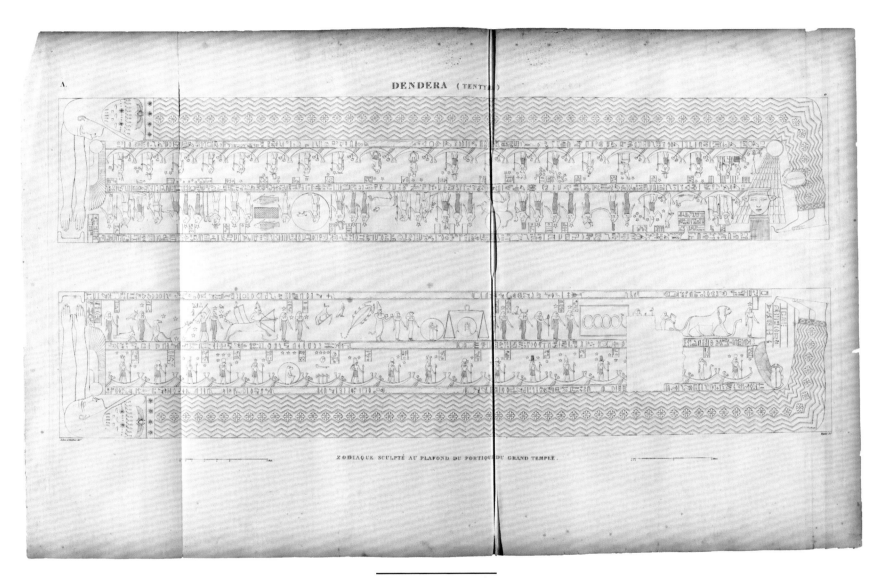

Outline from Description de l'Égypte, *vol. IV, plate 18, by Jollois and de Villiers.*

Also used as the outline for the panels on plate 20.

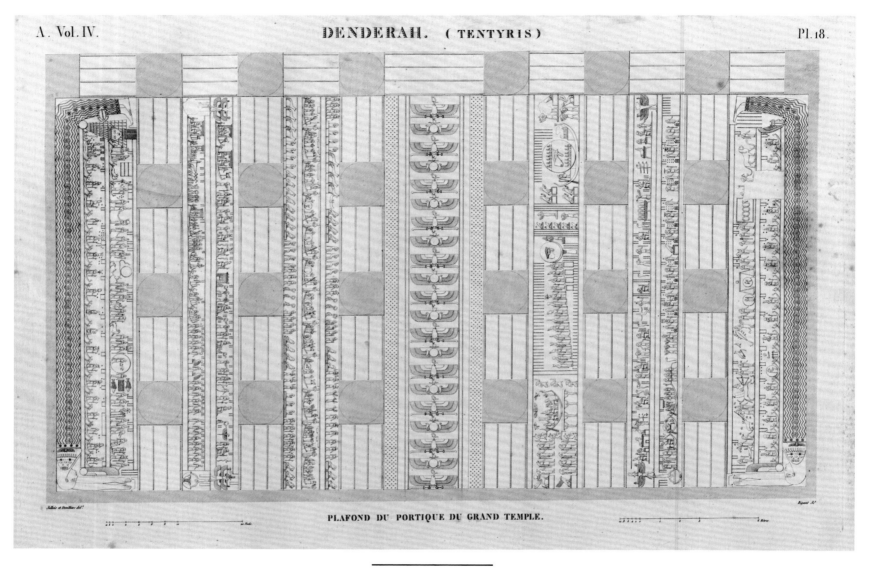

Reconstruction of the pronaos's ceiling of the temple of Dendera by Jollois and de Villiers from Description de l'Égypte, *vol IV, plate 19. Notice that Jollois and de Villiers struggled with the orientation of the image. They decided to show the north upward, so west and east are shown on the conventional sides. By doing so, the vultures on the central panel would have been upside down, unacceptable for the piece's aesthetics. They decided to take artistic license and flip them. Also, notice that there are not only vultures in the actual ceiling, but they alternate with cobra-headed vultures wearing the red crown of Lower Egypt. In this image, the winged solar disk is wearing the red crown. In reality, it wears the double crown, a symbol of the unification of Egypt.*

Bibliography

Allen, Richard Hinckley. 1899. *Star-Names and Their Meanings.* New York: G. E. Stechert.

Apuleius. 1998. *The Golden Ass or Metamorphoses.* London: Penguin Books.

Armour, Robert A. 2016. *Gods and Myths of Ancient Egypt.* Cairo: American University in Cairo Press.

Arnold, Dieter. 1999. *Temples of the Last Pharaohs.* Oxford: Oxford University Press.

Barton, Tamsyn. 2002. *Ancient Astrology.* London: Taylor & Francis.

Belmonte Avilés, Juan Antonio. 2012. *Pirámides, templos y estrellas: Astronomía y arqueología en el Egipto antiguo.* Barcelona: Crítica.

Blackburn, Bonnie, and Leofranc Holford-Strevens. 1999. *The Oxford Companion to the Year: An Exploration of Calendat Customs and Time-Reckoning.* Oxford: Oxford University Press.

Buchwald, Jed Z., and Diane Greco Josefowicz. 2010. *The Zodiac of Paris: How an Improbable Controversy over an Ancient Egyptian Artifact Provoked a Modern Debate between Religion and Science.* London: Princeton University Press, 2010.

Budge, E. A. Wallis. (1904) 2013. *The Gods of the Egyptians.* 2 vols. New York: Dover Publications.

———. (1911) 2012. *Osiris and the Egyptian Resurrection.* 2 vols. New York: Dover Publications.

Campion, Nicholas. 2012. *Astrology and Cosmology in the World's Religions.* New York: New York University Press.

Cauville, Sylvie. 1997. *Le Zodiaque d'Osiris: Le Zodiaque de Dendara au musée du Louvre* [The Zodiac of Osiris: The Zodiac of Dendera at the Louvre]. Louvain, Belgium: Peeters.

———. 1999. *L'œil de Rê: Histoire de la construction du temple d'Hathor à Dendara, du 16 juillet 54 av. J.-C. au printemps 64 ap. J.-C.* Paris: Pygmalion.

———. 2013a. *Dendara XV, Traduction: Le pronaos du temple d'Hathor, plafond et parois extérieures* [Ceiling and Outer Walls of the Pronaos of the Temple of Hathor]. Orientalia Lovaniensia Analecta. Louvain, Belgium: Peeters.

———. 2013b. *Dendara: Le pronaos du temple d'Hathor, Analyse de la décoration.* Orientalia Lovaniensia Analecta 221. Louvain, Belgium: Peeters.

Cauville, Sylvie, and Mohamed Ibrahim Ali. 2015. *Dendara: Itinéraire du visiteur.* Louvain, Belgium: Peeters.

Champollion, Jean-François. (1824) 1992. *Panthéon égyptien: Collection des personnages mythologiques de l'ancienne Égypte.* Paris: Inter-livres.

Chapman, Allan. 2002. *Gods in the Sky: Astronomy, Religion and Culture from the Ancients to the Renaissance.* United Kingdom, Channel 4.

Clagett, Marshall. 1989. *Ancient Egyptian Science: A Source Book.* Philadephia, Penn.: American Philosophical Society.

Clark, J. Desmond. 1984. *From Hunters to Farmers: The Causes and Consequences of Food Production in Africa.* Berkeley: University of California Press.

Clark, Robert Thomas Rundle. 1978. *Myth and Symbol in Ancient Egypt.* London: Thames and Hudson.

Condos, Theony. 1997. *Star Myths of the Greeks and Romans: A Sourcebook.* Grand Rapids, Mich.: Phanes Press.

Denon, Vivant. 1803. *Travels in Upper and Lower Egypt: During the Campaigns of General Bonaparte.* New York: Heard and Forman.

Diodorus, et al. 1933. *Library of History Volume 1.* Translated by C. H. Oldfather. Cambridge, Mass.: Harvard University Press.

Duncan, David Ewing. *The Calendar: The 5000-year Struggle to Align the Clock and the Heavens—and What Happened to the Missing Ten Days.* London, Fourth State.

Dupuis, Charles François. 1872. *The Origin of All Religious Worship.* New Orleans: n.p.

The Encyclopedia of Ancient Egypt. 2016. London: Amber Books.

Eratosthenes and Hyginus. 2015. *Constellation Myths: With Aratus's "Phaenomena."* Translated by Robin Hard. Oxford: Oxford University Press.

Faulkner R. O. 1938. "The Bremner-Rhind Papyrus-IV." *Journal of Egyptian Archaeology* 24, no. 1 (June): 41–53.

Gillispie, Charles C., and Michel Dewachter. 1987. *The Monuments of Egypt: The Napoleonic Edition.* Old Saybrook, Conn.: Konecky & Konecky.

Gleadow, Rupert. 2011. *The Origin of the Zodiac.* New York: Dover Publications.

Graves, Robert. 1959. *Larousse Encyclopedia of Mythology.* New York, Prometheus Press.

Herodotus. 1981–90. *Herodotus, Books I–IX.* Translated by A. D. Godley. Cambridge, Mass.: Harvard University Press.

Hoskin, Michael, ed. 1997. *The Cambridge Illustrated History of Astronomy*. Cambridge: Cambridge University Press.

Kanas, Nick. 2007. *Star Maps: History, Artistry, and Cartography*. Berlin: Springer.

Lockyer, J. Norman. (1894) 2006. *The Dawn of Astronomy: A Study of Temple Worship and Mythology of the Ancient Egyptians*. New York: Dover Publications.

Lull García, José. 2011. *La astronomía en el antiguo Egipto*. 2a ed. Valencia: Publicacions de la Universitat de València.

Magli, Giulio. 2013. *Architecture, Astronomy and Sacred Landscape in Ancient Egypt*. Cambridge: Cambridge University Press.

Mariette, Auguste. 1875. *Dendérah: Description générale du grand temple de cette ville*. Paris, Frank.

Maspero, Gaston. 1894. *The Dawn of Civilization: Egypt and Chaldæa*. London: Society for Promoting Christian Knowledge.

Massey, Gerald. (1907) 2011. *Ancient Egypt: The Light of the World*. United States, Createspace Independent Pub.

Mendel, Daniela. 2022. *Die Geographie des Himmels: Eine Untersuchung zu den Deckendekorationen in ägyptischen Tempeln der griechisch-römischen Zeit und zeitgleichen Darstellungen auf Särgen und in Gräbern*. Germany, Harrassowitz Verlag.

Mercatante, Anthony S. 1979. *Who's Who in Ancient Egyptian Mythology*. New York, Clarkson N. Potter.

Murray, Margaret A. (1931) 2002. *Egyptian Temples*. New York: Dover Publications.

Parker, R. A. 1874. *Ancient Egyptian Astronomy*. Philosophical Transactions of the Royal Society of London, Series A, *Mathematical and Physical Sciences* 276, no. 1257.

Pinch, Geraldine. 2004. *Egyptian Mythology: A Guide to the Gods, Goddesses, and Traditions of Ancient Egypt*. Oxford: Oxford University Press.

Plunket, Emmeline Mary. 1903. *Ancient Calendars and Constellations*. London: J. Murray.

Plutarch. 1927. *Plutarch's Moralia: V*. Cambridge, Mass.: Harvard University Press.

Priskin, Gyula. 2015. "The Dendera Zodiacs as Narratives of the Myth of Osiris, Isis, and the Child Horus. "*Égypte Nilotique et Méditerranéenne [ENiM]* 8 (Nov. 26): 133–85.

———. 2016. "The Depictions of the Entire Lunar Cycle in Graeco-Roman Temples." *The Journal of Egyptian Archaeology* 102. N.p.: Sage Publications.

Quack, Joachim Friedrich. 2019. "The Planets in Ancient Egypt." *Oxford Research Encyclopedia of Planetary Science*, https://doi.org/10.1093/acrefore/9780190647926.013.61.

Ragueh, Cherine Abou Zeid. 2016. "The Blessing of Grain Represented in God 'Nepri' and His Affiliate Gods of Grain: 'Osiris' and 'Renenutet.'" *Journal of the Association of Arab Universities for Tourism and Hospitality* 13, no. 2 (December).

Redford, Donald B. 2001. *The Oxford Encyclopedia of Ancient Egypt*. Oxford: Oxford University Press.

Rey, H. A. 2016. *The Stars: A New Way to See Them*. New York: Houghton Mifflin Harcourt Publishing Company.

Richards, Edward Graham. 1999. *Mapping Time: The Calendar and Its History*. Oxford: Oxford University Press.

Roberts, Alison. 1995. *Hathor Rising: The Serpent Power of Ancient Egypt*. Totnes, Devon, UK: Northgate, 1995.

———. 2019. *Hathor's Alchemy: The Ancient Egyptian Roots of the Hermetic Art*. Totnes, Devon, UK: NorthGate Publishers.

Robens, Erich, et al. 2013. *Balances: Instruments, Manufacturers, History*. Berlin: Springer.

Roth, Ann Macy. 2000. "Father Earth, Mother Sky, Ancient Egyptian Beliefs about Conception and Fertility." In *Reading the Body: Representations and Remains in the Archaeological Record*, edited by Alison E. Rautman. Philadelphia: University of Pennsylvania Press, 2000.

Sánchez Rodríguez, Ángel. 2000. *Astronomía y matemáticas en el antiguo Egipto*. Madrid, Alderabán Ediciones.

Shaw, Ian, ed. 2003. *The Oxford History of Ancient Egypt*. Oxford: Oxford University Press.

Silverman, David P. 2003. *Ancient Egypt*. Oxford: Oxford University Press.

Staal, Julius D. W. 1988. *The New Patterns in the Sky: Myths and Legends of the Stars*. Newark, Ohio: McDonald and Woodward Publishing Company.

Turner Cory, Alexander. 1840. *The Hieroglyphics of Horapollo Nilous*. London: Pickering.

Velde, Herman te. 1977. *Seth, God of Confusion: A Study of His Role in Egyptian Mythology and Religion*. Leiden: E.J. Brill.

Verner, Miroslav. 2013. *Temple of the World: Sanctuaries, Cults, and Mysteries of Ancient Egypt*. Cairo: American University in Cairo Press.

Villiers du Terrage, René-Edouard de, and Marc de Villiers du Terrage. 1899. *Journal et souvenirs sur l'expédition d'Égypte (1798–1801)*. Plon, France: Nourrit et cie.

Walker, Cristopher, ed. *Astronomy before the Telescope*. London: British Museum Press, 1996.

White, Gavin. 2014. *Babylonian Star-Lore: An Illustrated Guide to the Stars and Constellations of Ancient Babylonia*. London: Solaria Publications.

Wilkinson, Richard H. 1974. *Symbol and Magic in Egyptian Art*. London: Thames and Hudson.

———. 2003. *The Complete Gods and Goddesses of Ancient Egypt*. London: Thames & Hudson.

———. 2017. *The Complete Temples of Ancient Egypt*. London: Thames & Hudson.

Wilkinson, Sir John Gardner. (1923) 2014. *A Popular Account of the Ancient Egyptians: Illustrated with Five Hundred Woodcuts.* Vol. 2, Primary Source Edition. United States: BiblioLife, 2014.

Wilkinson, Toby. 2013. *The Rise and Fall of Ancient Egypt.* New York: Random House.

Zerubavel, Eviatar. 1989. *The Seven Day Circle: The History and Meaning of the Week.* Chicago: University of Chicago Press.

Zignani, Pierre. 2010. *Le temple d'Hathor à Dendara. Relevés et étude architecturale.* Vol. 1, Texte, vol. 2, Planches. Bibliothèque d'étude 146. Cairo: IFAO.

EXTERNAL IMAGES

Because hyperlinks do not always remain viable, we are no longer including URLs in our bibliographic entries. Instead, we are providing the details and name of the website where this information may be found.

P 18. Rare Book Division, New York Public Library. "Denderah [Dandara] (Tentyris). Vue de la porte du nord." The New York Public Library Digital Collections. 1817.

P 19. Rare Book Division, New York Public Library. "Denderah [Dandara] (Tentyris). Vue de la façade du Grand Temple." The New York Public Library Digital Collections. 1817.

P 20. Rare Book Division, New York Public Library. "Denderah [Dandara] (Tentyris). Vue générale des ruines prise de l'ouest." The New York Public Library Digital Collections. 1817.

P 21. Rare Book Division, New York Public Library. "Denderah [Dandara] (Tentyris). Vue perspective de l'intérieur du portique du Grand Temple." The New York Public Library Digital Collections. 1817.

P 54. General Research Division, New York Public Library. "Rappresentanze della camera funebre di Osiride [Osiris], relative alla sua morte e risorgimento." The New York Public Library Digital Collections. 1832–1844.

P 181. Rare Book Division, New York Public Library. "Denderah [Dandara] (Tentyris). Zodiaque sculpté au plafond de l'une des salles supérieures du Grand Temple." The New York Public Library Digital Collections. 1817.

P 183. Rare Book Division, New York Public Library. "Description de l'Égypte, . . . Antiquités. Planches. Tome première." The New York Public Library Digital Collections. 1809.

P 185, top. Rare Book Division, New York Public Library. "Zodiaque du plafond du portique de Tentyris [Dandara]." The New York Public Library Digital Collections. 1829.

P 185, bottom. Rare Book Division, New York Public Library. "Hieroglyphes qui sont au portique de temple de Tentyris [Dandara]." The New York Public Library Digital Collections. 1829.

P 186, top. Rare Book Division, New York Public Library. "Denderah [Dandara] (Tentyris). Zodiaque sculpté au plafond du portique du Grand Temple." The New York Public Library Digital Collections. 1817.

P 186, bottom. Rare Book Division, New York Public Library. "Denderah [Dandara] (Tentyris). Détail de quatre soffites du portique du Grand Temple." The New York Public Library Digital Collections. 1817.

P 187. Rare Book Division, New York Public Library. "Denderah [Dandara] (Tentyris). Zodiaque sculpté au plafond du portique du Grand Temple [Outline]." The New York Public Library Digital Collections. 1817.

P 188. Rare Book Division, New York Public Library. "Denderah [Dandara] (Tentyris). Plafond du portique du Grand Temple." The New York Public Library Digital Collections. 1817.

Index

Page numbers in *italics* refer to illustrations